UNIX SYSTEM ADMINISTRATION

Frank Burke

Middlesex County College
and
AT&T Information Systems

Harcourt Brace Jovanovich, Publishers
and its subsidiary, Academic Press

San Diego   New York   Chicago   Austin   Washington, D.C.
London   Sydney   Tokyo   Toronto

Copyright © 1987 by AT&T Information Systems, Inc.

All rights reserved. No part of this publication may be reproduced or transmitted in any form or by any means, electronic or mechanical, including photocopy, recording, or any information storage and retrieval system, without permission in writing from the publisher.

Requests for permission to make copies of any part of the work should be mailed to: Permissions, Harcourt Brace Jovanovich, Publishers, Orlando, Florida 32887.

Published simultaneously in Canada by Harcourt Brace Jovanovich Canada Inc., 55 Barber Greene Road, Don Mills, Ontario M3C 2A1, Canada.

ISBN: 0-15-593025-7
Library of Congress Catalog Card Number: 86-70500
Printed in the United States of America

The programs presented in this book have been included for their educational value. They have been carefully prepared but are not guaranteed. The publisher does not offer any warranties or representations with respect to the programs.

To my wife, Lee Ann, for her friendship,
to my daughter Karen for her determination,
to my daughter Ellen for her zest for life,
And to the memory of my parents.

CONTENTS

FOREWORD ix

PREFACE xiii

1. INTRODUCTION 1
   1.1 Where the System Administrator Fits into a UNIX Computer Center 1
   1.2 Suggested Reference Materials 2
   1.3 Prerequisite Knowledge 3
   1.4 Organization of the Book 4
   1.5 Conventions 4
   1.6 UNIX SYSTEM V 4

2. USER INTERFACE ADMINISTRATION 6
   2.1 Types of Computer Centers 6
   2.2 Information Transmission Commands 8
   2.3 Newsletter 15
   2.4 Education and Training of Computer Users 15
   2.5 Operations Room 16
   2.6 Summary 16
   2.7 Exercises 17

3. LOGIN ADMINISTRATION 19
   3.1 Steps in Setting Up a Login 19
   3.2 Authorization of Logins 20
   3.3 Selection of a Computer System 22
   3.4 Selection of a User File System 22
   3.5 Creation of the Password File Entry 23
   3.6 Case Study on Setting Up a Password File Entry 27

3.7	Creation of Associated Files and Directories	28
3.8	User Orientation	29
3.9	Automation of Login Set Up	29
3.10	Effect of Computer Center Size on Login Administration	29
3.11	Finding and Removing Obsolete Logins	31
3.12	Automation of Login Deletion	32
3.13	Protection of Login Information	32
3.14	Handling User Problems	32
3.15	Summary	32
3.16	Exercises	34

4. **DATA COMMUNICATIONS ADMINISTRATION** — 36

4.1	Review of Basic Concepts	36
4.2	Data Communications Software Overview	37
4.3	Data Communications Hardware Overview	38
4.4	Local Data Communications	41
4.5	Setting Up Ports on UNIX	42
4.6	Handling User Problems	44
4.7	Summary	45
4.8	Exercises	46

5. **FILE SYSTEM ADMINISTRATION** — 48

5.1	Review of Basic Concepts	48
5.2	What Is a File System?	51
5.3	Initial Set Up	55
5.4	Mounting and Unmounting File Systems	57
5.5	Sanity Checking	58
5.6	Backup	59
5.7	Maintaining File Systems	61
5.8	Summary	63
5.9	Exercises	63

6. **PROCESS ADMINISTRATION** — 66

6.1	What a Process Is	66
6.2	How Processes Are Created	67
6.3	Signals	68
6.4	Monitoring Processes	69
6.5	Killing Processes	73
6.6	Summary	74
6.7	Exercises	75

7.	OPERATIONS ADMINISTRATION	77
7.1	Designing an Operational Schedule	77
7.2	Implementing an Operational Schedule	80
7.3	Handling Emergencies	85
7.4	Operator Training	86
7.5	Summary	87
7.6	Exercises	88
8.	SECURITY ADMINISTRATION	90
8.1	Handling File and Directory Modes	91
8.2	Encrypting Files	95
8.3	Controlling Superusers	96
8.4	Managing Logins	97
8.5	Enhancing Password Security	97
8.6	Limiting Telecommunications Access	98
8.7	Limiting Tape Production	99
8.8	Computer Room Security	99
8.9	Summary	101
8.10	Exercises	102
9.	ADMINISTRATION OF COMPUTING RESOURCES	104
9.1	Resource Administration Objectives	104
9.2	Monitoring Free Space	105
9.3	Monitoring Cpu Usage	106
9.4	Monitoring Ports	109
9.5	Identifying Bottlenecks	112
9.6	Solving Computing Resource Problems	114
9.7	Summary	115
9.8	Exercises	115
10.	PLANNING A SYSTEM CONFIGURATION	117
10.1	Components of a Hardware Configuration	117
10.2	Typical Configurations	121
10.3	Preparing a Bid Specification	124
10.4	Obtaining Your System	127
10.5	Site Preparation	127
10.6	Summary	127
10.7	Exercises	129

11.	**SYSTEM GENERATION OVERVIEW**	131
11.1	Hardware Configuration	131
11.2	Documentation	132
11.3	Prerequisites	133
11.4	The Emergency Action Interface	133
11.5	Initial Loading and Booting	135
11.6	Initial Load of /usr File System	137
11.7	Initial Load of Selectable Items	137
11.8	Special Files	138
11.9	System Description File	141
11.10	Making UNIX	142
11.11	Summary	143
11.12	Exercises	144
12.	**NETWORK ADMINISTRATION**	145
12.1	Network Introduction	145
12.2	User Interface Commands	146
12.3	Hardware Overview	148
12.4	Program Overview	149
12.5	File Overview	150
12.6	Setting Up *Uucp*	153
12.7	Security Considerations	155
12.8	Solving User Problems	155
12.9	Summary	156
12.10	Exercises	156
13.	**ADMINISTERING CHANGE**	158
13.1	Converting to a New UNIX Release	158
13.2	Augmenting Host Hardware	160
13.3	Bringing Up New Host Hardware	162
13.4	Moving Computers	164
13.5	Summary	165
13.6	Exercises	166

APPENDIX A: REFERENCES	169
APPENDIX B: MANUAL PAGES REFERENCED	171
INDEX	173

FOREWORD

My first job after graduation was as a system administrator in a large computer center. We had a large multiprocessor Honeywell system running GCOS, a Cray-1 running COS, and "those three little white machines in the back of the room" running UNIX. I was the UNIX administrator. The Cray pretty much ran itself with little operator intervention. The GCOS system required a lot of operator coverage — one or more operators were dedicated to watching the console. The UNIX systems also tended to need a fair amount of operator coverage, but they didn't get it. Not too many people took them very seriously. These systems — the hardware and the operating system — were so small in comparison to the big mainframes that they weren't expected to need a lot of attention.

UNIX system administration was quite a bit different in those days. There were rumors of a course that one could take but few did. There certainly wasn't any written material besides the *man* pages found in the UNIX System User Reference Manual. No, the only the way a *real administrator* learned was by doing. You found another system administrator and watched while he or she reorganized the file systems or installed new releases of the UNIX system. When it was your turn you would study all the *man* pages for *volcopy, labelit, mkfs, find,* and *cpio*. You might spend ten hours on a Saturday evening copying files and making mount points until midnight when, bleary eyed after staring at a slow console for so long, you execute a *mkfs* with the wrong arguments. Before your finger could travel those three and a half centimeters from the return key to the break key you realize in the pit of your stomach that the last ten hours of work have been destroyed.

Eventually the new system administrator gets over his or her fears of superuser. One of the first things they always seem to do of their own volition is rewrite the backup and login administration programs. Most distributed versions of UNIX do not come with these programs. Invariably, these shell scripts were written by the former system administrator, but they just don't do what is really required.

UNIX System Administration removes the necessity to learn system administration by example only. You will learn the reasons why file systems are reorganized, not just the mechanics. For example, in Chapter 3 you'll learn all the steps required to set up a new login from a suggested standard login form to the files that need to be modified. At the end of the chapter there is an example of a new user program that may be similar (but not as custom tailored) to the one running at your site. Chapter 4 on data communications may not seem immediately appropriate but it is. Even if you have a separate data communications staff at your site, you will be required to understand in fair detail RS232 protocol so that you can help debug problems associated with connecting your UNIX tty ports to other devices.

Some of the chapters in this book necessarily delve into the operating system. The UNIX administrator needs to know something about how the file system is implemented (Chapter 5) in order to effectively do those reorganizations to improve system performance or repair file system damage. Similarly, Chapter 9 on *Administration of Computing Resources* explains the *sar* command and the internal variables that it monitors. An understanding of how the operating system does process management is also necessary for effective performance improvements.

If you do not work in a computer center but are reading this book to learn how to build one, Chapters 10 and 11 can help you. They explain the whole process from the initial planning to vendor selection to system installation to bringing up the very first UNIX image.

Each chapter begins with a list of objectives and ends with exercises so you can practice what you learn. By the time you finish this book, you'll be ready to take on any kind of UNIX system. But be careful. There's still no experience like practical experience.

Oh, by the way — that computer center I described earlier.... Well, I started working there a mere five years ago. By now they are running UNIX on ten *small* systems, on two IBMs, an Amdahl, and one-half of a CRAY-XMP.

Steven B. Goldsmith
March 1986

PREFACE

I entered the UNIX* world in 1977, when Middlesex County College bought its first UNIX system and gave me the assignment of bringing it up and integrating it into our academic program. Our first system was brought up under UNIX Version 6 and later under UNIX 3.0. I first developed course modules on 'C' and shell in 1978. These modules were followed by a full semester 'C' course in 1979 and a full semester shell course in 1983. The college then granted me a sabbatical to develop our new UNIX System Administration course. The course was first taught in the Fall semester of 1985, and the notes for that course eventually became this textbook. I have been a SYSTEM V† user since its announcement and have focused the book on SYSTEM V.

SYSTEM V and lookalikes have been ported to many different vendors' hardware. Although *UNIX System Administration* is targeted primarily at minicomputer-sized systems, it will be useful in the range from personal computers to mainframes. My experience has been on AT&T (UNIX PC, 3B2, and 3B20), Digital Equipment Corporation (PDP11§ and VAX), Amdahl (5860), and Pyramid (90X) hardware.

Who This Book Is for

The primary objective of this book is to educate UNIX system administrators. Each major job function of a UNIX system administrator is discussed. The intended level is the fourth semester of a computer science degree program.

---

* UNIX is a registered trademark of AT&T Bell Laboratories.
† SYSTEM V, UNIX PC, 3B2, and 3B20 are registered trademarks of AT&T.
§ PDP11 and VAX are registered trademarks of Digital Equipment Corporation.

The topics covered in this book exhibit some overlap with the functions of a UNIX operator. The operations tasks covered are those with which administrators commonly become involved. No attempt has been made to provide complete coverage of the knowledge and skills required of a computer operator.

The education of a UNIX system programmer usually includes a bachelor's degree in computer science plus vendor-specific courses on hardware and operating system structure. While this book may be of interest to a potential UNIX system programmer, its thrust is not in the system programming area.

Need for a System Administration Course

The UNIX System Administration course at Middlesex County College was designed at the request of the college's computer science industrial advisory committee to address a perceived severe shortage of UNIX system administrators within the college's service area. The course was part of a complete curriculum redesign that also added a required UNIX shell course. Because of the shortage of UNIX system administrators, the Department of Higher Education of the State of New Jersey granted the college $105,000 to set up a laboratory in support of the UNIX System Administration course. The laboratory also received support from the AT&T UNIX Enhancement Program.

Pedagogy

UNIX System Administration contains the following teaching aids:

1. A list of objectives at the start of each chapter
2. Numerous examples of UNIX system administration problems and solutions
3. A summary at the end of each chapter
4. An exercise set at the end of Chapters 2-13
5. Appendix A, an annotated list of UNIX reference books; and Appendix B, a list of UNIX manual pages referenced

A teacher's manual is available containing answers to exercises, sample tests, a sample examination, and advice on hardware dependencies.

Acknowledgments

I am indebted to several organizations and a large number of individuals. Middlesex County College provided me with a sabbatical during which much of this book was written. In particular, I would like to acknowledge the support and encouragement of Deans Frank Spano and Warren Kelemen and Professor John Dineen. Professors Paul Bhatia and Timothy Muenzer taught UNIX System Administration using the manuscript and offered many helpful suggestions.

In the early days of bringing up UNIX at Middlesex College, I had productive discussions with Dick Haight, Ralph White, Mary Ellen Pearlman, and Ken Thompson of AT&T Bell Laboratories. Bob Pajauis, initially our laboratory coordinator and currently our UNIX system programmer at Middlesex College, has been a valued colleague and source of sound advice.

AT&T has played a key role in my professional development over the past decade. Trude Stetter, head of the Shore Systems Department at AT&T Bell Laboratories, has served on the college's industrial advisory committee for many years and has been instrumental in keeping us on the leading edge of UNIX technology. I spent a summer teaching PDP11 architecture and assembly language at the AT&T Education Center in Princeton, New Jersey, two summers as a UNIX counselor for the AT&T Bell Laboratories Holmdel, New Jersey Computer Center, and five summers doing 'C' and shell software development and computing resource planning for the AT&T Integrated Systems Division (formerly part of Bell Laboratories, now part of AT&T Information Systems). I wish to thank the management of the Integrated Systems Division for providing the rich technical environment and well focused challenge that have brought me to the point of writing this book. In particular, A. Feiner, C. D. Weiss, C. S. Roberts, T. L. Warner, J. E. Ritacco, D. K. Coursen, and G. S. Yates have been supportive of professional development.

During my summers at AT&T Bell Laboratories and AT&T Information Systems, many productive relationships have developed. Tom Pedersen has always been willing to provide help on many diverse issues. Steve Goldsmith has shared his experience as a 3B20 system administrator and his comprehensive knowledge of UNIX. Evelyn Leeper has been a valued source of system administration information on numerous occasions.

I have had a pleasant and effective working relationship with my editor, Dale R. Brown, and his administrative assistant, Carollee Kaba. Dale has kept me headed in the right direction and has helped me make good use of the time I have available to write the book. Carolee kept the editorial process running smoothly and at a brisk pace. The assistance of Karen Bierstedt, Director of Editorial, Production, and Design for Academic Press, was timely, professional, and appreciated. I am also grateful to Richard Bonacci, Computer Science Editor of Harcourt Brace Jovanovich, for his assistance.

I have been fortunate to have a varied panel of industrial and collegiate reviewers to help perfect the manuscript. The industrial reviewers were: Steve Goldsmith, Supervisor of Computing Technology (UNIX System Administration), AT&T Information Systems; Denise Coursen, Member of Technical Staff, AT&T Bell Laboratories, and Bob Pajauis, UNIX System Administrator, Middlesex County College. The collegiate reviewers were: Professor R. Page, University of Lowell; Professor J. F. Peters III, St. John's University, Collegeville, Minnesota; Professor R. Valensawalia, Trenton State College; and Professor J. Youhonas, University of Alabama at Huntsville.

Last, but not least, I would like to thank my wife, Lee Ann, and my daughters, Karen and Ellen, for being patient with me during the many hours I have spent writing and word processing this book. My wife also gave me the benefit of her training as an English teacher in keeping my grammatical errors at a manageable level.

1. INTRODUCTION

UNIX System Administration is designed to educate UNIX* system administrators. Chapter 1 describes where the UNIX system administrator fits into a UNIX computer center. Then, reference materials are listed, the prerequisite knowledge for successfully using this book is specified, and the organization and syntax convention of the book are described. Finally, the specific software and hardware used for illustration in the book are specified.

1.1 Where the System Administrator Fits into a UNIX Computer Center

The three major job classifications in a large UNIX computer center are: (a) operator, (b) system administrator, and (c) systems programmer.

1.1.1 Operator

A UNIX operator's job consists of performing a substantial number of tasks that repeat on a periodic basis such as: (a) bringing up a system, (b) shutting down a system, and (c) doing file backups.

The operator's job is typically learned through on-the-job training.

1.1.2 System Administrator

UNIX system administrators obtain, set up, and maintain UNIX systems. In a large computer center, UNIX system administrators may supervise UNIX operators who work under their technical direction. In a small computer center, the UNIX

---

* UNIX is a registered trademark of AT&T Bell Laboratories, Inc.

system administrator may also be the UNIX operator.

UNIX system administration is a professional level job. To a large extent, the specific tasks that may be required on a given day are unpredictable. When a job arises, it may require quick, accurate judgment. Some things that a UNIX system administrator may do on a given day are:

1. Check with operations to be sure all the systems came up satisfactorily and that the file backup tapes were made.

2. Write a shell program to determine the number of users on each system.

3. Install a new software package.

4. Diagnose a system problem.

5. Schedule a vendor to install a new disk drive.

1.1.3 System Programmer

A computer center may also have one or more UNIX system programmers. These highly trained professionals may do the following jobs:

1. Modify device drivers

2. Create new device drivers

3. Modify the UNIX kernel

1.2 Suggested Reference Materials

The following manuals are referenced in this book. You should have a copy of these manuals available:

1. *UNIX System V Release 2.0 Administrator Reference Manual,* AT&T Bell Laboratories, Inc., 1983.

2. *UNIX System V Release 2.0 Programmer Reference Manual,* AT&T Bell Laboratories, Inc., 1983.

3. *UNIX System V Release 2.0 User Reference Manual,* AT&T Bell Laboratories, Inc., 1983.

1.3 Prerequisite Knowledge

UNIX System Administration is written for readers who have completed the equivalent of three semesters of undergraduate work in computer science. It is assumed that you have had courses or experience equivalent to Introduction to Computer Science and Data Structures. It is also assumed that you have knowledge of UNIX shell programming corresponding to Chapters 1-5 of *The UNIX Programming Environment* by Kernighan and Pike or equivalent. Equivalent knowledge is as follows:

1. Familiarity with the commonly used *Unix User's Manual* section 1 commands, including:

    cat

    cd

    chmod

    cp

    grep

    ls

    mail

    mkdir

    ps

    pwd

    rm

    rmdir

    who

2. Knowledge of an editor such as *vi*
3. Understanding of and ability to use input and output redirection and pipes
4. Understanding and ability to use shell metacharacters and variables
5. Experience writing small shell programs

Knowledge of 'C' language is not assumed.

1.4 Organization of the Book

Chapter 2 discusses establishing an effective relationship with the users of a UNIX system. Chapters 3, 4, 5, and 6 discuss the provision of the following basic resources of a UNIX system:

1. Logins
2. Ports
3. File systems
4. Processes

The remainder of the book discusses the following job functions of a system administrator:

1. Supervising operations
2. Securing the system
3. Monitoring and controlling system use
4. Planning software conversions
5. Planning a system configuration
6. Doing system generation and tuning
7. Running a network
8. Planning for change

Appendices include a selected UNIX bibliography and a list of manual pages relevant to the topics covered in the book.

1.5 Conventions

The following conventions will be used in this book:

1. Names of commands will be shown in italic type.
2. Names of files will be shown in boldface type.
3. Optional arguments will be enclosed in square brackets.
4. Repetition will be shown with an ellipsis.

1.6 UNIX SYSTEM V

This book is based on UNIX SYSTEM V, Release 2. The Bourne shell is used for illustration.

The book is approximately 80 percent hardware independent. In the limited number of cases in which it is necessary to include a specific hardware illustration, the AT&T 3B family or Digital Equipment Corporation family of minicomputers is used.

2. USER INTERFACE ADMINISTRATION

OBJECTIVES

After reading this chapter, you should be able to:

1. Name the major types of computer centers.
2. Explain the value of user representatives.
3. Set up the "message of the day."
4. Set up "news" items.
5. Send and read electronic mail.
6. Send broadcast messages.
7. Choose an appropriate information transmittal approach for each administrative purpose.
8. State the major topics that a computer center newsletter would contain.
9. Explain the job of a computer center program counselor.
10. Explain the purpose of a computer center operations room.

A computer exists to serve its users. Therefore, the administrator of a UNIX system must have good channels of communication available to the user community.

2.1 Types of Computer Centers

Computer centers can be classified as "public" or "private." A "public" computer center is one that is run by the central administration of a company or university. A "private" computer center is usually run by the organization that uses it.

2.1.1 Public Computer Centers

In a public computer center, the management of the computer center makes decisions as to the type of hardware and software to be supported. Users are generally spread out in small groups over a large organization with diverse needs and interests. The public computer center maintains a staff of experts who determine the direction that the computer center will take. User consultation does not necessarily play a dominant role in the decision making process, and users may find that they adapt to the type of services provided rather than control the requirements for these services.

2.1.2 Private Computer Centers

A private computer center may exist specifically to serve the needs of one university department or one business organization. The organization served usually owns the computers and controls the requirements for provision of computing resources.

The use of "user representatives" is one approach to setting requirements for computing resources. A "user representative" is a person who can speak for the users of a computer. On a large mainframe, each user department may have a user representative so that there may be several representatives for the computer. Typically, a minicomputer will serve only one department or group and will have one user representative.

Major changes to a computer's hardware, software, or operational procedures might be discussed with the user representative for that computer. For example, if your computer had to be down on a Saturday for an equipment upgrade, the user representative could help you pick the Saturday that would be the least disruptive for the user community.

One of the important documents that system administrators of a private computer center maintain is a list of their computers, user representatives, room numbers, and phone numbers.

2.1.3 Public Versus Private Computer Centers

Public computer centers achieve economy of scale. Private computer centers respond quickly to the user organization's needs. Each type of computer center has its place in a modern business organization.

Some areas of system administration are handled differently in public and private computer centers. These areas will be explicitly identified as such at appropriate points in the book.

2.2 Information Transmission Commands

The information transmission commands and methods to be discussed here are "message of the day," news, electronic mail, and broadcast messages.

2.2.1 Message of the Day

The "message of the day" (motd) is a message that UNIX automatically displays to each user at login time. It is used as a means of passing on routine information to all users of a computer. For example, a Saturday shutdown for equipment upgrade might be announced by the message of the day for Thursday or Friday. Figure 2.1 shows two messages of the day. The first message of the day simply identifies the system. The second message of the day identifies the system and announces the availability of a new phototypesetter.

In order to put up a message of the day you create a file named **motd** under the /etc directory. The *login* program displays the **motd** file on the standard output as each user logs on. This file is displayed to every user during every login process.

2.2.2 News

Users may use the *news* command to read news items posted by UNIX administrators. The *news* command displays selected information about files in the /usr/news directory. News is useful for routine information that may be of interest to some but not all users of a computer.

A systems administrator creates a news item by editing a file in the /usr/news directory.

Message 1:

Welcome to the Blue UNIX System.

Message 2:

Welcome to the Blue UNIX System.
Type:
news IMAGEN
to find out how to use the new phototypesetter.

Figure 2.1   Sample Messages of the Day

The *news* command has considerable flexibility, including the following options:
1. <no arguments> displays the contents of current news files with a header
2. -a displays the contents of all news files
3. -n displays the names of news files
4. -s displays the number of news files

One common approach is to put the command:

news -n

in the **/etc/profile** file. The **/etc/profile** is executed every time someone logs into a UNIX system. This has the effect of displaying the names of all news items to all users as they log in.

Figure 2.2 shows the creation and display of a news item regarding an approaching shutdown. The system administrator

Command placed in **/etc/profile** by administrator:

news -a

Contents of **downtime** file placed in **/usr/news** directory by administrator:

The "Blue" UNIX system will be down Saturday from 8 A. M. until 2 P. M. for the installation of additional memory and disk drives.

Screen of each terminal during login:

The "Blue" UNIX system will be down Saturday from 8 A. M. until 2 P. M. for the installation of additional memory and disk drives.

Figure 2.2   Sample News Item

would edit the **/etc/profile** file and insert the command

    news -a

to cause all news files to be displayed during login and would create the **downtime** file with an appropriate message in the **/usr/news** directory. The **downtime** file would then be displayed to users the next time they logged on.

2.2.3 Electronic Communications Services

Electronic mail and bulletin boards can significantly enhance the speed and reliability of communication. Electronic mail packages commonly perform the following tasks:

1. Send electronic mail
2. Read electronic mail
3. Post electronic bulletin boards
4. Read electronic bulletin boards

Electronic mail could be used to ask user representatives if a certain date is a good time for a shutdown for equipment upgrade. An electronic bulletin board for each computer could be used to keep that computer's user community informed of plans for the computer. Electronic mail is used when information must be transferred quickly. Electronic bulletin boards are comparable to news items in terms of the amount of time it takes for information to get to users. Basic electronic mail is provided with UNIX SYSTEM V. Enhanced electronic communications may be purchased as an add-on program package.

Basic Electronic Mail

The *mail* command is used to send electronic mail. For example

```
$mail joe
<message>
^d
$
```

will cause the message to be sent to login 'joe.' ^d means that the control and 'd' keys are pressed at the same time.

The *mail* command is also used to read electronic mail. It is invoked with no argument to read mail. When the *mail* command is executed your first mail message will be displayed. Some of the *mail* subcommands are:

<CR> — (carriage return) displays the next message.

s — saves the mail in your mailbox (mbox).

d — deletes the mail.

w file_name — writes a copy of the mail message
to the specified file.

Mailx is another command used for sending and reading mail.

Enhanced Electronic Communications

Electronic bulletin boards allow quick communication to various interest groups within a user community. Users may examine a list of available bulletin boards and subscribe only to those that are of interest to them. You will need to purchase an add-on package to gain this capability, however. The major advantage of electronic bulletin boards is that you can establish multiple boards and inform only a subset of the user community when appropriate. If your computer center had several computers, you could create a bulletin board for the users of each computer, for example.

2.2.4 Broadcast Message

A broadcast message is a message that is displayed immediately to all users who are logged into a computer. It is used to disseminate information of an urgent nature, for example an imminent emergency shutdown of a computer. The broadcast message will appear in the middle of any program output going to the screens of user terminals. Because this is the most disruptive method of communicating with users, it should be used sparingly.

One way to send a broadcast message is by first creating a file containing the message and then using the *wall* command with standard input redirected to come from the message file. Figure 2.3 illustrates how to send a broadcast message from a file.

Command:

$ *wall* <shutmsg

$

Contents of **'shutmsg'** file:

System coming down in 5 minutes!!!
Please log off.

Display Screen of All Terminals Logged into the System:

System coming down in 5 minutes!!!
Please log off.

Figure 2.3   Broadcast Message from a File for an Emergency Shutdown

Another way to send a broadcast message is directly from the terminal keyboard. Figure 2.4 illustrates how to send a broadcast message from a terminal.

2.2.5 Choice of Information Transmission Method

Various information transmission commands and methods have been described. The choice of an information transmission command depends on the urgency of the information conveyed. Table 2.1 lists the various electronic means of transmitting information, together with the typical information transmission time for each command or method. News and message of the day are used for nonurgent information. Electronic mail and broadcast messages are used for urgent information.

Command:

$ *wall*

System coming down in 5 minutes!!!
Please log off.

^d

$

Display Screen of All Terminals Logged into System:

Broadcast message from root on console

System coming down in 5 minutes!!!
Please log off.

Figure 2.4   Broadcast Message from a Terminal for Emergency Shutdown

Table 2.1   Overview of Information Transmission Commands and Methods

COMMAND	INFORMATION CLASS	TIME FRAME
News	Nonurgent	Next Login
Motd	Nonurgent	Next Login
Mail	Semiurgent	Minutes
Broadcast	Urgent	Seconds

2.3 Newsletter

A periodically distributed newsletter can be a vehicle to pass information to users. For example, a newsletter could be used to provide information on telephone and room numbers of key personnel, new operating system releases, charging rates, new software packages, planned hardware upgrades, and personnel changes. Although the newsletter could be printed and distributed to people on a mailing list, a more efficient method of distribution would be to make an on line copy available. A *newsletter* command might be provided by the system administrators as follows:

> *cat* /usr/newsletter | *pg*

A "public" computer center will generally have a newsletter in order to notify users about important hardware and software changes. A "private" computer center might have a newsletter but probably will rely on more informal methods of communication.

2.4 Education and Training of Computer Users

The education and training function can be broken down into one-on-one program counseling and group-based education and training.

2.4.1 Counseling

A "counselor" is someone who helps users to effectively use computing resources. Generally a large "public" computer center will set up a counseling office and publish the name, telephone number, and room location of the counselor. In a "private" computer center, one or more advanced UNIX users generally become counselors on an informal basis. Some of the things a counselor might help users with are:

1. Differences between the current UNIX release and an upcoming release
2. Orientation of new users

3. The telephone numbers of various computers
4. Use of a new software package
5. Correction of a billing error
6. Programming help
7. Text processing help

A good counselor will become the focus of user questions and problems. An administrator should be able to explain a new package or the solution to a problem to a counselor once, and the counselor would then pass the information on to numerous users.

2.4.2 Group-Based Education and Training

There may be times when it is appropriate to schedule a short seminar on a new or underutilized system feature. Likewise, when a new release of UNIX comes out, a seminar on changes in the release might be helpful. In many cases the UNIX system administrator is in a position either to conduct the seminar or to obtain someone who can conduct it.

2.5 Operations Room

The operations room is a place where the computer operators can be reached. Users need to know the room number and telephone number of the operations room. Users should be instructed to call the operations room when they want a tape read in, if they have mistakenly removed a file and need to have it restored from a backup tape, or if they need other operational help.

2.6 Summary

There are two major types of computer centers: a "public" computer center serves a whole college or industrial organization; a "private" computer center serves a single college department or industrial organization. The two types of computer center have different needs for user communication.

Private computer centers may have user representatives to provide information on user needs. Public computer centers rely on a program counseling office or aid station to learn the needs of their users.

System administrators use several UNIX commands to communicate with users. The "message of the day" is displayed to users as they log on. The administrator puts the "message of the day" in the /etc/motd file.

The administrator can have the system display complete news items or the names of news items when users log in by placing a *news* command with an appropriate argument in the /etc/profile file. The administrator places the news files themselves in the /usr/news directory.

Electronic mail is sent and read using the *mail* command. Mail can be sent to a specific user.

Broadcast messages are sent using the *wall* command and are immediately displayed on every user's screen. Because these messages are displayed in the middle of user output, they are highly disruptive.

A computer center newsletter may be used to communicate nonurgent information to users. Changes to charging rates and new software packages might be announced in this fashion.

Publishing the telephone number and room number of a computer center operations room allows users to obtain current information on the operational state of their computer and any needed help. Users may want a file restored from a backup tape, a tape read in, or a software distribution tape made.

2.7 Exercises

1. What would you do if you were the user representative for a computer system and were asked if your computer could be taken down Saturday to add an additional megabyte of memory? How would you assess the positive and negative effects of this change on your user community?

2. Post a "news" item announcing that a new line printer is available for use in room 1d235 that can be accessed using

    lp -d a

3. Describe what you would do to make every news item appear on every user's screen when he or she logged on.

4. Set up a message of the day that announces the system name and release of UNIX and welcomes the user to your college.

5. Send electronic mail to your professor telling him or her that you have read this chapter.

6. Investigate the electronic bulletin boards facility provided at your institution. What advantages do electronic bulletin boards have over *news*?

7. Show the command that you would use to tell all the users of a system that the system is coming down in 5 minutes.

8. What method of transmitting information would you use in the following cases?

    The computer must come down in two minutes for a reboot.

    A new phototypesetter will be available for use next month.

    The system will be down next Saturday morning to add more memory.

9. Prepare a newsletter outline for a computer center that has one minicomputer and serves a community college.

10. Make a list of several questions that you had when you first started using your computer that would be appropriate to ask a program counselor.

11. Explain the effect of the various arguments of the *news* command.

3. LOGIN ADMINISTRATION

OBJECTIVES

After reading this chapter, you should be able to:

1. Set up effective procedures for the authorization of login names (logins).
2. Explain the use of each field in an entry in the /etc/passwd file.
3. Set up a login.
4. Know how to manage logins properly in a computer center containing several UNIX systems.
5. Set up effective procedures for removing logins for people who no longer should have them.
6. Help users who are unable to log on.

Logins are an important method of limiting the use of a computer to authorized persons. The system administrator sets up procedures for administering logins on a system. The actual administration of logins may be done by the administrator, an operator, or a clerk.

3.1 Steps in Setting Up a Login

The several steps involved in setting up a login on a UNIX system are:

1. The login must be authorized.
2. A computer system must be selected to host the login.
3. A file system must be selected in which to place the login directory for the login.

4. The login entry must be appended to the **/etc/passwd** file.
5. The login directory for the login must be made.
6. The **.profile** file for the login should be set up.
7. The user may be given a document indicating how to get started.

3.2 Authorization of Logins

Determining who should be given a login on a computer is a management function. A document should exist that clearly specifies who is allowed to authorize logins. A login should be authorized in writing on a standard form, and the form should be retained for as long as the login is allowed to remain in effect. Normally, the authorizer of the login shares responsibility with the system administrator for ensuring that the login is used in an appropriate fashion.

A sample login request form is shown in Figure 3.1. Sections identify the user, provide for approval of the login, and log the set up of the login.

3.2.1 Public Computer Center

In general, any employee of a company should be able to get a login in a public corporate computer center. The computer center will have procedures to verify that the person is a valid employee, which might involve checking with the personnel department.

In a university environment, any student should be able to get a login. The computer center will have procedures to verify that the person is a valid student, which might involve checking with the registrar's office.

3.2.2 Private Computer Center

Generally, a manager reviews requests for logins. Authorization of logins for members of the organization owning the computer would be routine. Authorization of logins outside the organization that owns the computer on which the login is to reside is a special case. Outside logins may be necessary, but their existence should be known to several members of management.

USER DATA

NAME _____

ROOM NUMBER _____

LOCATION _____

PHONE NUMBER _____

PREFERRED COMPUTER NAME _____

I agree to use my login according to company policy.

SIGNATURE _____   DATE _____

SUPERVISORY APPROVAL

Please set up the above login for:

A. My employee

B. The person named above

(circle one)

I agree to be responsible for the use of the above login in accord with company policy.

SUPERVISORY SIGNATURE _____

COMPUTER CENTER USE ONLY

COMPUTER CENTER SIGNATURE _____
(Required for outside logins)

PERSON SETTING UP LOGIN _____ DATE _____

Figure 3.1   Sample Login Request Form

3.3 Selection of a Computer System

If your computer center has only one computer, selecting the computer is easy. In a computer center with several computers, a choice must be made. Users may express a preference for a certain computer on their login request form. The system administrator determines if resources on the preferred computer are available and assigns the login to that computer or an appropriate alternate. The *sar* -u command provides data on whether or not a system has spare cpu capacity.

3.4 Selection of a User File System

A file system is a subset of a disk. Logically, the file system includes all the files and directories below a certain point in the UNIX file tree structure, such as /a1. On a given computer system, one or several file systems may contain user files.

To determine the available disk resources in a file system, the system administrator uses the *df* command. For example, if the system administrator wants to determine if adequate disk resources remain in file system /a1, then he or she uses the command:

    df   /a1

This command reports the amount of space (in blocks) and the number of additional files that can be created there. Block size is hardware dependent and is either 512, 1,024, or 4,096 bytes.

In a public computer center, new users can be placed in any file system that has disk resources. Users known to be working together on the same project are usually grouped together. In a private computer center, users are usually placed in a file system with other members of their work group, provided there are sufficient disk resources.

Proper organization of login directories facilitates monitoring disk usage and balancing of users. Disk I/O slows down considerably in a nearly full file system. A rule of thumb is not to place additional users in a file system that has less than 20 percent of its original resources available. For example, in a 500 K block file system, no additional users

LOGIN ADMINISTRATION

should be added when less than 100 K blocks are available. In order to determine the initial and current available resources of a file system, the -t argument is used on the *df* command.

3.5 Creation of the Password File Entry

In this section, the /etc/passwd file format will be described. Then, setting up the individual fields of the password file entry will be explained. Finally, an example of setting up a password file entry will be presented.

3.5.1 Password File Structure

The /etc/passwd file specifies authorized logins in UNIX. There is a one-line entry per login. The fields in the login entry are separated by ':'s. At times a field may be null and appear as '::'. The format of a login entry is:

   login:passwd:UID:GID:comment:directory:shell

where:

1. Login is the login name.

2. Passwd initially holds a code specifying the requirement for the installation of a password and, after password installation, holds the code and the encrypted password.

3. UID is the user identification number, an integer between 0 and 65,535, that identifies the user to UNIX.

4. GID is the group identification number, an integer that identifies the group to UNIX.

5. Comment usually describes the person(s) responsible for the login in human-readable form.

6. Directory is the login directory, the place in the UNIX hierarchical file system where this user will be placed at the completion of the login process.

7. Shell is the login shell that will be spawned on completion of the login process. The shell is the UNIX "user interface."

3.5.2 Advice on Password File Entries

Login Name

One convention for naming logins is to use the initials of the user. In the case of F. J. Burke, the initials are 'fjb.' Having login names correspond to users' initials makes life easier for administrators in many ways. For example, users currently logged on may be identified, as may the owner of a file.

In many organizations several users might have the same initials. For example, a user named Fred J. Berk might be assigned login 'fred' or login 'berk.'

Some logins are traditionally assigned a functional name, such as rje, uucp, and so on. The effort in setting up easily identifiable, mnemonic login names will be quickly paid back.

Password

The system administrator initially sets up the password field. The initial setting of this field determines whether or not a password will be required for the login and what the parameters of its expiration will be.

The encrypted password is computed later by the *passwd* program using input from the user. The encrypted password has 13 characters selected by *passwd* from the character set:

(., /, 0-9, A-Z, a-z)

The initial password field format can be either of the following:

1. ,<max char><min char>
2. <null>

where <max char> and <min char> are defined below and <null> is a null field (nothing). The characters <max char> and <min char> are chosen from the following alphabet:

(., /, 0-9, A-Z, a-z)

The character . corresponds to 0, / corresponds to 1, and z corresponds to 64 weeks. The first 8 character codes and the corresponding number of weeks is shown in Table 3.1.

An encrypted password must be changed within the time frame specified by <max char>. An encrypted password must not be changed any more frequently than the time frame specified by <min char>. For example, to force an encrypted password to be used and changed at least every 8 weeks and no more frequently than every 4 weeks, we would put

',62'

into the password field. The maximum time specification is '6', which indicates 8 weeks. The minimum time specification character is '2', which indicates 4 weeks. Automatic password expiration is sometimes called password "aging."

User ID
The user ID (UID) is an integer that identifies a user to UNIX. The UID is used by UNIX to determine the ownership of files and processes. If two logins had the same UID, UNIX would be unable to distinguish between them. Use a UID that has not been used for another user. One approach is to start user UIDs at 100 and number /etc/passwd entries sequentially. Thus if 150 was the UID of the last entry made in the /etc/passwd file, the next user would be assigned UID 151. UIDs 0 and 65,536 have "superuser" privileges and should not be assigned to ordinary users.

Group ID
The group ID (GID) is an integer that identifies the user's group. Group permissions of a file are determined by the file's GID. Giving everyone the same GID allows everyone group privileges on all user files.

A group is a subset of the user community. A UNIX group may correspond to an administrative group or may be a subset or superset of an administrative group. Generally groups are defined by community of interest. All the people working on one project might be assigned to the same group. Although some harried administrators assign every ordinary

Table 3.1   Password Expiration and Change Codes

Character	Weeks
.	0
/	1
0	2
1	3
2	4
3	5
4	6
5	7

user to the same group, this practice is undesirable from a security standpoint.

Comment Field

The comment field should contain information that is helpful to the administrator. One approach is to include the name associated with this login and the name of the responsible supervisor for the login. A code could identify someone who is an outside user. This information could be taken from the login request form.

Login Directory

The login directory is the directory in which the login program places the user at the completion of the login process. In addition to specifying the login directory in this field, you must also create the login directory. Login directories are created in one or more user file systems.

Login Shell

The last field is used by the login program to determine the login shell that is to be given to the user. Many different shells are available. The administrator makes a default choice for his or her users. Usually this choice is **/bin/sh.** A null login shell field may be used to specify **/bin/sh.**

3.6 Case Study on Setting Up a Password File Entry

The problem is to set up a login given the following requirements:

1. The login is for John J. Doe.
2. The login is to have an encrypted password. The password is to expire monthly. The password is to be changed no more frequently than weekly.
3. The UIDs from 0 to 105 have already been used.
4. The GID of John Doe's group is 50.
5. John J. Doe's supervisor is F. P. McGarry.
6. The login directory is to be under the /al file system.
7. The login shell is to be /bin/sh.

A suitable login entry in /etc/passwd for this user is shown below:

jjd:,2/:106:50:j.j.doe(f.p.mcgarry):/a1/gp1/jjd:/bin/sh

Note the following:

1. John J. Doe's initials are 'jjd.' Since a password file search shows that no other login exists with these initials, 'jjd' will be the login name.
2. We put the characters

    ',2/'

   in the password field. The ',' indicates that a password must be used. The '2' indicates that the user will be forced to change the password every 4 weeks. The '/' indicates that, once changed, the password must remain in effect for at least a week.
3. Since UIDs 0-105 have already been used, the UID for this login will be 106.

4. The GID for this login will be 50 to match the other people in this user's administrative group.

5. The comment field will be

   j.j.doe(f.p.mcgarry)

6. The login directory will be **/a1/gp1/jjd**. **Gp1** is an existing directory. **Jjd** is a directory created manually at the time the login is set up.

7. The shell field will be **/bin/sh**. This is the full path name of the standard shell.

3.7 Creation of Associated Files and Directories

It is necessary to make the login directory, **.profile** file, and mail file for the new login.

3.7.1 Login Directory

The login directory is made as specified in the new user's password file entry. Ownership of the login directory is changed to the new user's login name.

3.7.2 The .profile File

The **.profile** file is executed when a user logs on and customizes the user's login session to his or her needs. The system administrator creates an initial version of this file under the new user's login directory and changes ownership of the file to the user. The PATH shell variable is initialized in the user's **.profile** file to the value that specifies the standard places in which the installation keeps commands. For example, the following assignment statement might be placed in a new user's **.profile** file:

   PATH=:/bin:/usr/bin:/usr/local/bin

A sample **.profile** file is shown below:

   PS1="SYSTEM_A: "

PATH=:/bin:/usr/bin:/usr/local/bin

3.7.3 Subdirectories

We have the option of creating commonly used subdirectories for the user. For example, **rje** and **bin** subdirectories might be created under the login directory. The **bin** subdirectory is used for the user's private commands. The **rje** subdirectory is used by file transfer commands.

3.8 User Orientation

New users may be given a short memo containing the phone number of their computer, the phone number to call for help, and other pertinent information.

3.9 Automation of Login Set Up

Figure 3.2 shows a basic shell that will set up a login. The shell prompts the administrator for the new user's name, the desired login name, desired file system, UID (user identification number) and GID (group identification number). The shell appends an **/etc/passwd** entry, makes the user's login directory, gives ownership of the login directory to the user, and gives the user a **.profile** file.

The shell shown in Figure 3.2 is designed to illustrate the basic operations involved in login set up. In an operational environment there would be protection against unintentional hangup or hitting of the break key during shell execution.

3.10 Effect of Computer Center Size on Login Administration

A computer center may have one UNIX system or several. Procedures for administering logins are affected by the number of UNIX systems that a computer center has.

In the case of a single UNIX system there is only one password file and login administration is straightforward.

Login administration becomes somewhat more complex when there are several machines in a UNIX computer center. Some users may want the same login name to exist on several machines. It is also necessary to keep track of which users

Obtain Data for Login

echo "Enter user name"

read N

echo "Enter desired login name"

read L

echo "Enter desired file system"

read F

echo "Enter desired UID"

read U

echo "Enter desired GID"

read G

Make login directory

mkdir $F/$L

Provide default .profile

cp /usr/adm/proto/.profile $F/$L

Append password file entry

echo "$L:,:$U:$G:$N:$F/$L:" >> /etc/passwd

#Change Login Directory Ownership

chown $L $F/$L

chgrp $G $F/$L

Figure 3.2   Sample Login Set Up Shell Program

have logins on the various machines.

Unique UIDs and GIDs Across Machines

A login name that exists on several machines should have the same UID and GID on all machines. UNIX uses UID to identify a user and GID to identify a group. If the same login name had different UIDs on different systems, UNIX would not be able to recognize files as belonging to the same owner if they are moved between systems.

Master System

One machine could be the focal point of login management. A recent copy of the password files from all computer center machines could be kept in a directory on that machine. Then when we need to determine on what machine or machines a login resides, we would only have to look in one place.

3.11 Finding and Removing Obsolete Logins

Obsolete logins may be found by examining a file that contains the date of last login or through a procedure by which the personnel department notifies the computer center when a user leaves the company. It is relatively easy to purge an obsolete login and related files and directories.

The file /usr/adm/acct/sum/loginlog contains information on logins and the date and time of the last login. Logins that have not been used for several months should be investigated to determine if they should be removed.

A procedure could be set up whereby the personnel department notifies the computer center when an employee leaves. Supervisors should also be encouraged to call the computer center when an employee leaves.

In order to remove a login, the following action needs to be taken:

1. Remove the password file entry.
2. Remove the login directory.
3. Remove the mail file.
4. Remove the /usr/spool/uucppublic directory for the user.

3.12 Automation of Login Deletion

Figure 3.3 shows a sample login deletion shell. It prompts the operator or system administrator for the login name to be deleted and the file system name containing the login directory, displays the login entry to be deleted, and requests confirmation that the user wants to proceed. Given confirmation, the login entry, login directory, and mail file are deleted. Given denial, the shell terminates.

3.13 Protection of Login Information

If the /etc/passwd file were destroyed, no ordinary user would be able to log on. For this reason a copy of the /etc/passwd file should be kept on line under a different name.

3.14 Handling User Problems

Users who are unable to log on will contact an administrator. Sometimes the problem is as simple as a forgotten password. In this case the administrator resets the password field for the login and the user is advised to log on and install a new password. Setting the password field to ',62' will allow the installation of a new password and enforce password aging.

Sometimes a user is unable to log on because there is no password file entry for the user. The administrator can use an editor or the **grep** command to determine if an entry exists for the user in the /etc/passwd file. If there is no password file entry for an authorized user, one is installed.

Sometimes a user is unable to log on because there is no login directory. Checking for the presence of the specified login directory is the second step in analyzing login problems. If the login directory does not exist, or is not owned by the user, the administrator makes the login directory or changes ownership of the directory to the user as appropriate.

3.15 Summary

Login names are used to limit computer system access to authorized users. Customarily, users fill out a form to apply for a login name and a management-defined criterion is applied by the administrator to determine if the login name, also called login, is set up. Login names are normally protected by

Obtain Login Data

echo "Enter login to be deleted"

read L

echo "Enter file system name containing login directory"

read F

Confirmation

echo "You will be deleting the following"

grep "^$L:" /etc/passwd

echo "Do you want to continue"

read R

if $R = y

Remove the login

then

rm -r $F/$L

rm /usr/mail/$L # mail file

sed '/^$L:/d' /etc/passwd > /tmp/passwd

cp /tmp/passwd /etc/passwd

Quit

else

exit (1)

fi

Figure 3.3   Sample Login Deletion Shell Program

passwords to prevent unauthorized use.

The system administrator creates a login by making an entry in the **/etc/passwd** file. The password entry has a login name, password, user identification (UID), group identification (GID), comment, login directory, and login shell fields.

UIDs and GIDs are integers that identify the user and group associated with a file or process. A login must be known by the same UID across all systems that it resides on if UNIX is to properly determine file and process ownership for the login.

Logins are removed when users leave an organization.

When users forget their passwords, the system administrator must reset their password field. Sometimes users will be unable to log on for other reasons. An administrator will use the *grep* command or an editor to examine the **/etc/passwd** file entry for the login as the initial step in problem analysis.

3.16 Exercises

1. Show the **/etc/passwd** entry that you would use to create a login for yourself.

2. Describe how you would locate and examine the **/etc/passwd** file entry for login 'fjb.'

3. Write a shell program that will print out all the **/etc/passwd** entries that contain the supervisor's name 'jones.'

4. Write a shell program that will print the **/etc/passwd** file entries that do not have passwords.

5. Write a shell program that will list the logins that have not been used this year.

6. How could the sample login set up shell program be improved?

7. How could the sample login deletion shell program be improved?

8. Write a shell program that takes a login name as input and outputs the file system name containing the

LOGIN ADMINISTRATION 35

associated login directory.

9. Write a shell program that outputs the number of /etc/passwd file entries.

10. Explain why you might want to keep a duplicate copy of the /etc/passwd file. Where would you suggest keeping it?

11. A user calls and reports an inability to log in. What would you do to help resolve her problem?

4. DATA COMMUNICATIONS ADMINISTRATION

OBJECTIVES

After reading this chapter, you should be able to:

1. Understand basic data communications terminology.
2. Name the processes involved in the login scenario.
3. List the hardware needed to support communications to a terminal.
4. Make appropriate file entries to set up a communications port.
5. Deal with user problems relating to data communications.

Users communicate with UNIX using terminals in a data communications environment. This chapter explains how to set up a suitable data communications environment.

Some basic data communications terms will be explained; then overviews of the software and hardware used in the UNIX data communications environment will be given. The special case of the computer and terminal being in close proximity will be discussed. Then a procedure to set up UNIX data communications ports will be presented. Finally, some hints on dealing with user data communications problems will be given.

4.1 Review of Basic Concepts

We use the term "data communications" to refer to the transfer of data from a terminal to a computer and vice versa. In UNIX, data communications to a terminal are full duplex (data may be sent and received concurrently). Data communications may be switched over phone lines or carried over hard wired lines. UNIX communications to a terminal are asynchronous, meaning transmission is done a character at a time, whenever the character is available.

4.2 Data Communications Software Overview

Four types of UNIX processes execute sequentially to set up a communications channel between a user terminal and a UNIX multiplexer port. Figure 4.1 shows these four processes. The processes are *init*, *getty*, *login*, and *sh*. Each of these processes will be described.

4.2.1 Init Process

Init is a general purpose process spawner. It reads a script in /etc/inittab and spawns processes as requested. *Init* recognizes several run levels, or states. It spawns a set of processes for each state. Two important states are single user and multi-user. In multi-user state, *init* spawns a *getty* process for each port listed in /etc/inittab.

4.2.2 Getty Process

A *getty* process is spawned for each communications port when a system goes from single user to multi-user mode. *Getty* outputs a login prompt onto a terminal screen (or printer) and reads the login name typed by a user on the terminal keyboard. *Getty* then invokes the *login* program. A *getty* is spawned with a specific data communications port number as an argument, and it attaches to this port. A default line speed can be provided as an optional argument to a *getty* process.

4.2.3 Login Process

The *login* process starts a terminal session. It asks for your password and, if correct, executes the */etc/profile* and *.profile* shell programs. Finally, *login* spawns a *sh* (shell) process for the terminal session.

4.2.4 Shell Process

A shell process provides UNIX command interpretation and provides a user interface. *Sh* is one common shell. It implements the UNIX command language as specified on the *sh* manual page.

The specific shell to be spawned is determined by the login shell field in the **/etc/passwd** file entry matching the login name.

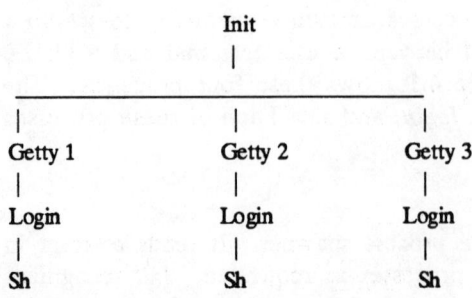

Figure 4.1   Data Communications Software Overview

4.3 Data Communications Hardware Overview

The three main elements of the UNIX data communications hardware configuration are:

1. terminals
2. multiplexer ports
3. data transmission media

Figure 4.2 shows a block diagram of UNIX data communications hardware. Each of the elements of this block diagram will now be discussed.

4.3.1 Terminals

UNIX uses 128 character ASCII (American Standard Code for Information Interchange) asynchronous terminals. These terminals are operated in full duplex mode. The terminals usually have an Electronic Industries Association (EIA) RS232C interface to data communications equipment. Transmission speed and other UART (Universal Asynchronous Receiver Transmitter) parameters are set on the terminal by switch or keyboard control. Many manufacturers make

DATA COMMUNICATIONS ADMINISTRATION

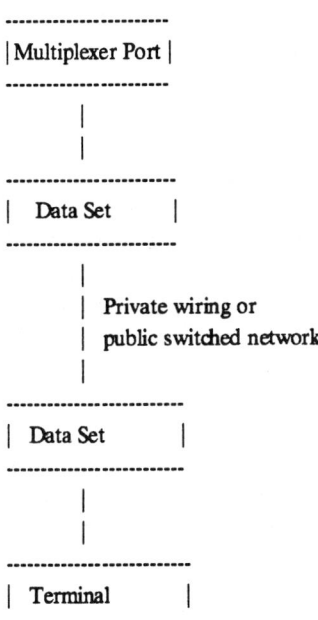

Figure 4.2   Data Communications Hardware Overview

terminals meeting the above requirements.

4.3.2 Multiplexer Ports

The multiplexer ports on the UNIX system usually also have the EIA RS232C interface to data communications equipment. These ports operate asynchronously in full-duplex mode. The transmission speed and other UART parameters are under software control.

4.3.3 Data Sets

Asynchronous data sets provide the capability to transmit data from one point to another over private wiring or the public switched phone network. A data set is also called data communications equipment and would normally have an EIA RS232C interface.

4.3.4 Transmission Medium

The transmission medium gets the data from one point to another. The medium originally consisted of a twisted wire pair. Today the medium could be a twisted wire pair or could be a microwave, coaxial cable, or optical fiber communications channel. This medium is available both on the public switched network and on a point-to-point basis. The interface to this medium is typically a modular jack that plugs into a data set.

4.3.5 RS232C Interface

Computer equipment such as a multiplexer port or data terminal typically interface with data communications equipment (data sets or modems) using the Electronics Industries Association (EIA) RS232C interface.

The RS232C interface is a formal specification of a standard interface between a data set (or modem) and computer equipment such as a terminal or multiplexer port. The data set is termed data communications equipment (DCE). The terminal and multiplexer port are termed data terminal equipment (DTE). The data transmission medium is termed the communications channel.

This interface is physically implemented in a 25 pin male or female connector. In practice, only a few of the 25 pins are used. Table 4.1 illustrates commonly used pin numbers and functions. If you examine the face of an RS232C connector carefully, you will see small numbers next to the pins or holes; these are the pin numbers. The Signal Ground pin provides an electrical reference point. The Transmitted Data pin has data the computer or terminal wants the data set to transmit over the communications channel. The Received Data pin has data received by the data set over the communications channel.

The Request to Send pin is used by the terminal or port to condition the local data communications equipment (DCE)

Table 4.1 Commonly Used Pins on the RS232C Interface

Pin Number	Function
2	Transmitted Data
3	Received Data
4	Request to Send
5	Clear to Send
6	Data Set Ready
7	Signal Ground
8	Received Line Signal(Carrier) Detect
20	Data Terminal Ready

for data transmission. The state of readiness of the data set to transmit data is indicated by the Clear to Send pin. The Data Set Ready pin indicates that the data set has power and is in data mode. The Received Line Signal (Carrier) Detect signal is presented by the local DCE when it is receiving a suitable signal on the communications channel. The Data Terminal Ready signal is used by the terminal and computer port to prepare the local DCE to be connected to the communications channel.

Monitoring and Debugging on the RS232C Interface

A number of companies manufacture monitoring and debugging instruments for the RS232C interface. These instruments are commonly called "break out boxes." They have a male and a female RS232C connector built in and contain indicators that show the status of each signal in Table 4.1. Some of them also contain a set of switches and jumpers that allow any signal to be forced on or off. Having one of these instruments available is a considerable help in debugging RS232C interface problems.

4.4 Local Data Communications

When a terminal and a multiplexer are within several hundred feet of each other, data communications can function without data sets. In this case an eight-wire cable is run between the terminal and multiplexer and a "null modem" connector is used in place of the data sets. A wiring diagram for a "null modem" is presented in *Technical Aspects of Data Communication*, by John McNamara (Digital Press, Bedford, MA, page 209). "Null modems" are readily available from computer accessory dealers.

4.5 Setting Up Ports on UNIX

Two files play a key role in setting up data communications ports on UNIX.

1. /etc/inittab
2. /etc/gettydefs

The /etc/inittab file controls the action of the *init* process and the /etc/gettydefs file controls the behavior of the *getty* processes. These files will now be described.

4.5.1 /etc/inittab

The /etc/inittab file controls the action of the *init* process. The inittab file contains entries in the following format:

id:rstate:action:process

Id is simply an ASCII label. Rstate is the number of the state in which a *getty* is to be spawned. Two important states are 1 (single user) and 2 (multi-user). Action is the class of action to be taken. Common actions are off (no process is spawned) and respawn (a process will be respawned if it no longer exists). Process is the process to be spawned and is usually /etc/getty with port number and baud rate arguments. The -t <timeout> option can be used to have *getty* exit if nothing is typed on a line in <timeout> seconds.

Baud is the number of signals per second. If there is one bit transmitted per signal, then 1200 baud is equivalent to 1200 bits per second (bps), which is equivalent to 120 characters per second. Data communication over normal dial up telephone connections is at 300 or 1200 baud. Data communication over specially conditioned lines or hard wired lines can also be at 2,400, 4,800, 9,600, or 19,200 baud.

DATA COMMUNICATIONS ADMINISTRATION

A sample /etc/inittab file is presented in Figure 4.3. In Figure 4.3 the first line is for the system console. This line is given the label 'co.' The second argument is '0126' indicating that the process is to be spawned for run states 0, 1, 2, and 6. The action is respawn and the process is /etc/getty with argument console. This process will attach to the console.

The second line of Figure 4.3 is for an ordinary port. The label on the second line is 00. The run state is 2, or multi-user. The action is respawn and the process is /etc/getty with arguments tty00 and 1200. This process will try to attach to tty00 and attempt to communicate at 1200 baud.

4.5.2 /etc/gettydefs

The /etc/gettydefs file controls the action of the *getty* processes. The format of the /etc/gettydefs file is as follows:

label#initial-flags#final-flags#login-prompt#next-label

Each entry must be followed by a blank line.

Generally, the /etc/gettydefs file distributed in a UNIX release will be adequate for most users. It will not be necessary to edit the /etc/gettydefs file unless an unusual piece of equipment must be set up on the system.

Label is the string against which *getty* tries to match its second argument. It is usually the speed at which the terminal is expected to run. Initial-flags are the *ioctl* settings to which the terminal type is set if the terminal type is not specified to the *getty* process. *Ioctl* is a function used to control character special files (devices). Final-flags are set just before the *getty* process executes the *login* process. Login-prompt is the character string printed as the login prompt. Next-label is the next entry in the **gettydefs** file to be used if the current entry does not specify the correct speed. A break character from the terminal will send *getty* to search the next label.

Figure 4.4 shows a sample /etc/gettydefs file. The first entry is labeled 300 and is for a terminal operating at 300 baud. If the terminal speed is not 300 baud, the 1200 entry is tried.

```
co:0126:respawn:/etc/getty console console
00:2:respawn:/etc/getty tty00 1200
01:2:respawn:/etc/getty tty01 1200
02:2:respawn:/etc/getty tty02 9600
```

Figure 4.3   Example of **/etc/inittab**

The 1200 entry is for a terminal operating at 1200 baud. If the terminal baud rate is not 1200 baud, the 300 line is tried.

Table 4.2 shows the meaning of the values for initial-flags and final-flags shown in Figure 4.4. In Table 4.2 three columns are shown. The first column contains the flag value. The second column specifies the direction to which the flag pertains (I = input, O = output, I/O = input and output). The third column explains the meaning of the flag.

4.6 Handling User Problems

One common problem in data communications is mismatched transmission speeds between a terminal and a computer port. The problem displays itself as "garbage" characters on the terminal screen instead of the normal login message. Often, the transmission speed mismatch can be solved by hitting the "break" button on the terminal, causing the computer port to cycle to the next transmission speed specified in the **/etc/gettydefs** file.

If a user is trying to communicate at a transmission speed not supported by your **/etc/gettydefs** file, you can edit the file to include the new transmission speed, provided the computer port hardware is capable of operating at that speed. Otherwise, the user needs to adjust the terminal's data communications configuration to specify a transmission speed supported by the computer hardware.

Another common problem occurs when a user gets a busy signal after attempting to access the computer in a dial up environment. The system administrator can execute the *who*

300 # B300 IGNPAR ISTRIP ICRNL ONLCR OPOST ECHO ICANON ISIG CS7 #
B300 SANE # <nl><cr> logon: # 1200

1200 # B1200 IGNPAR ISTRIP ICRNL ONLCR OPOST ECHO ICANON ISIG CS7 #
B1200 SANE # <nl><cr> logon: # 300

Figure 4.4   /etc/gettydefs Example

command to determine the number of users logged on to a computer and compare that number to the number of installed computer ports. Perhaps additional ports are needed or users need to be encouraged to log off when they will be away from their terminals for long periods of time. Alternatively, some broken ports might need to be repaired.

A user who dials the computer, hears a carrier (a high pitched tone), or gets other confirmation of the connection being made and gets no further response probably has found a broken port. A technician should be asked to check the computer's ports.

4.7 Summary

The *init* process spawns other UNIX processes, including *getty* processes, when UNIX goes from single user to multi-user state. A *getty* process for each data communications port tries to log a user onto the port by spawning a *login* process when input comes in on the port. When a *login* process receives a correct login name and password, a *sh* process is spawned and the user is logged on.

Users communicate with UNIX using a terminal. The terminal can be connected to a data set or a hard wired line. UNIX computer ports likewise can be connected to data sets or hard wired lines. UNIX communicates with terminals in full duplex mode in an asynchronous fashion.

Table 4.2 Terminal Handling Flags

VALUE	DIRECTION	MEANING
B300	I/O	Baud rate is 300
B1200	I/O	Baud rate is 1200
IGNPAR	I	Ignore parity
ISTRIP	I	Strip character to 7 bits
ICRNL	I	Map CR to NL
ONLCR	O	Map NL to CR-NL
OPOST	O	Postprocess output
ECHO	I	Enable echo
ICANON	I	Enable erase and kill processing
ISIG	I	Enable signals
CS7	I/O	7 bit characters
SANE	I/O	Set parameters to reasonable values

A system administrator sets up a data communications port by making an entry in the /etc/inittab file containing port name, active state, and process to be attached to the port. The /etc/gettydefs file contains generic specifications on how the ports will be treated and generally does not need to be changed.

4.8 Exercises

1. What are the four processes involved in logging a user into UNIX?

2. What hardware is needed to support data communications to a terminal?

3. Name three of the commonly used pins on the EIA RS232C interface connector and describe the use of each.

4. Explain the difference in the required data communications hardware configuration for local versus long distance communication.

5. What is baud?

6. What file would you edit so that a login session would get a shell other than *sh?* What process spawns the shell?

DATA COMMUNICATIONS ADMINISTRATION

7. Show the /etc/inittab entry for tty72, which is to be operated at 4800 baud.

8. Modify Figure 4.4 to make the *getty* cycle from 1200 baud to 2400 baud and then to 300 baud.

9. What would you tell users who are getting "garbage" characters instead of a login prompt when they try to log on?

10. When a user dials the computer and gets a "busy" signal, how can you verify that it is caused by an insufficient number of ports on the computer?

11. What would you do if a user was trying to communicate with the system at a transmission speed that was not listed in /etc/gettydefs?

5. FILE SYSTEM ADMINISTRATION

OBJECTIVES

After reading this chapter, you should be able to:

1. Explain the concept of a hierarchical file system.
2. Have a basic understanding of UNIX file systems.
3. Set up a new file system.
4. Mount and unmount a file system.
5. Sanity check a file system.
6. Back up a file system.
7. Handle routine file system maintenance.

Files are an important resource on a computer system. In UNIX, files are organized in file systems. A UNIX system administrator sets up and maintains the file systems.

5.1 Review of Basic Concepts

The three major classes of files in UNIX are: (a) regular, (b) directory, and (c) special. Each of these types of files will be briefly described along with the concept of a hierarchical file system.

5.1.1 Regular File

A file is a sequential stream of bytes. In the 3B computers and most other popular computers a byte is 8 bits. A byte can contain an ASCII (American Standard Code for Information Interchange) character or 8 bits of machine language. No format is imposed on a file in UNIX. A file is simply a sequence of bytes. Some examples of regular files are:

FILE SYSTEM ADMINISTRATION

INUMBER	NAME
2 Bytes	14 Characters

Figure 5.1   Directory Format

1. A collection of characters corresponding to a source program
2. A collection of characters corresponding to the input data for a program
3. A machine language program

5.1.2 Directory

The concept of a directory is a fundamental part of the UNIX hierarchical method of organizing files. A directory is a file that contains entries with a specific format. The format is a two byte inumber followed by a 14 character name. Figure 5.1 shows the format of a directory.

The inumber is the number of the inode for this directory entry. The 14 character name is the name of the directory entry. The name is null padded and left justified within its field. In UNIX, the inode contains the information needed by the operating system for this directory entry. The directory entry may be for a regular file, another directory, or a special file.

The presence of an entry for a file in a directory means that the file is contained in that directory. Directories impose a hierarchical file system structure in UNIX.

5.1.3 Hierarchical File System

The file systems in UNIX look like an inverted tree diagram. Directories define the tree structure. Each directory may contain files or other directories or both. For example, in Figure 5.2 the / directory contains the **usr, etc,** and **al** directories and the **memo** file. The names shown in parentheses in Figure 5.2 are regular files. The other names are directories.

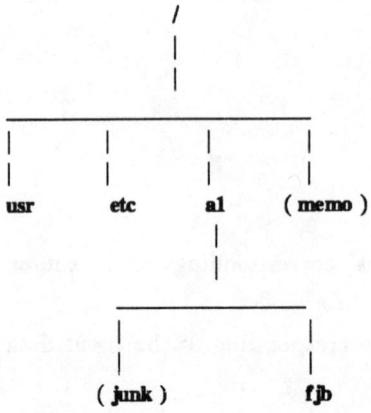

Figure 5.2   Hierarchical File System Example

5.1.4 Special File

A special file is an interface to a device driver for a peripheral device. The inode for the special file contains a specification for the device including:

1. An indication as to whether the device is a block or character oriented device

2. The major device number for the device (an integer uniquely identifying the type of device)

3. The minor device number for the device (an integer uniquely identifying a particular device or request for specific device action)

Examples of special files are **mt0** (a tape drive), **tty20** (a terminal), and **null** (an imaginary device used as a "bit bucket").

5.2 What Is a File System?

Before addressing the actions required of a system administrator to maintain file systems, we will investigate the organization of a UNIX file system. The innovative UNIX approach to utilizing disk storage provides more flexibility and user transparency than traditional methods of organizing files. The following important concepts underlie the UNIX file system:

1. Blocks
2. Pointers to blocks
3. A free list
4. Inodes
5. The superblock
6. Device format

These concepts are important, not only from the standpoint of abstract computer science, but also as a basis for understanding how UNIX organizes files in file systems.

5.2.1 Blocks

The concept of addressing a disk by a block number rather than by a track and cylinder number originated in minicomputer hardware that was used for the early versions of UNIX. Blocks are contiguous groups of bytes that have a unique address. On early hardware the size of a block was 512 bytes, but now the size may be 1,024 or 4,096 bytes, depending on the specific hardware that hosts UNIX. What is important is not the block size but the idea of a contiguous group of bytes on a disk that can be accessed with a single address. In UNIX, each disk drive is viewed as an array of blocks.

5.2.2 File Implementation in UNIX

UNIX implements a file as a group of one or more pointers to disk blocks. The pointers are stored in the control block for the file (called inode), which will be discussed later. The UNIX operating system provides blocks to hold the data when a file is created and takes back blocks when a file is removed in a manner that is transparent to users. This method is totally unlike traditional methods of file creation in which a user must have detailed knowledge of the location of free disk space.

For example, consider a 600 byte file. UNIX provides two blocks (assuming a block size of 512 bytes), and a pointer to each of these blocks is stored in the file control block for the file.

5.2.3 The Free List

Blocks not currently being used to hold the information for a file are held in a linked list, called a free list. Initially, all the data blocks of a disk drive are on a free list. When blocks are needed for use in a file they are removed from the list. When they are no longer needed for use in a file, they are added to the list. Figure 5.3 shows a small part of a free list. The free list starts at the location pointed to by the free list pointer, and each node has a pointer to the next node or else has a sentinel pointer to mark the end of the list. Each node contains the block numbers of several free blocks.

5.2.4 Inodes

The file control block in UNIX, called the inode, is manipulated by UNIX in a manner that is transparent to the ordinary user. A UNIX inode contains all essential information about a file except its name, which is stored only in the directory containing the file. The number of the inode is called the inumber of the file. The following fields are in an inode:

1. Mode and type of file
2. Number of links to the file
3. Owner's user ID
4. Owner's group ID
5. Number of bytes in the file
6. Array of disk block addresses
7. Last access time
8. Last modified time
9. Time of last status change

In UNIX SYSTEM V each inode contains 13 disk block

FILE SYSTEM ADMINISTRATION

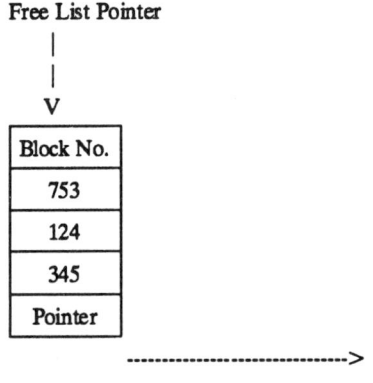

Figure 5.3   A Free List

addresses, which are each three bytes long. Ten addresses are for direct access, the eleventh is for indirect access, the twelfth is for double indirect access, and the thirteenth is for triple indirect access.

5.2.5 Superblock

A superblock is a control block for a collection of UNIX files, called a file system. There is one superblock per file system. The superblock contains:

1. The file system name
2. The name of the disk pack holding the file system

Boot block or unused
Superblock
start of ilist
end of ilist
start of data
end of data

Figure 5.4 File System Disk Format

3. The number of inodes that the file system was created with

4. The number of data blocks that the file system was created with

5. The number of currently free inodes

6. The number of currently free blocks

7. A pointer to the start of the free list

8. Other control information used for reasons of efficiency or synchronization

A copy of the superblock is maintained in memory and on disk. UNIX periodically updates the disk copy of the superblock for each file system. If the administrator is about to bring the system down, the *sync* command can be used to force UNIX to update the disk copy of the superblock for each file system.

5.2.6 File System Device Format

Each file system contains four major parts: (a) boot block (sometimes unused), (b) superblock, (c) ilist, and (d) data blocks. The format of the file system on a device is shown in Figure 5.4, where block 0 is either the boot block or unused and block 1 is the superblock, followed by the inodes and ending with the data blocks.

5.3 Initial Set Up

This section describes how file systems are initially set up. First, a decision must be made regarding what file systems to create and on what disk drive to place each file system. Second, the commands necessary to create the file systems must be executed.

5.3.1 Mapping File Systems to Disk Drives

The setting up of file systems is hardware dependent. You need to determine what model disk drive you have and look up the data on that drive in section 7 of the *UNIX System Administrator Reference Manual*. Table 5.1 shows information on the Digital Equipment Corporation RP07. The table shows the configuration that has been set up for the RP07 drive by UNIX SYSTEM V. For example, section 0 is special file **rp070**, which starts at cylinder 0 and is 64,000 (512 byte) blocks long. Cylinders on the RP07 are 1,600 blocks long. Note that most of the sections shown in Table 5.1 overlap and that you might only set up one file system on the drive (namely, section 7), or you might set up two file systems on the drive (namely, sections 0 and 1).

5.3.2 Creating a New File System

After we decide on the section to use we issue two commands to set up a new file system: the */etc/mkfs*, and */etc/labelit* commands.

The */etc/mkfs* command is issued to make a file system. A slightly simplified version of its syntax is:

    /etc/mkfs   special_file   blocks

"Special_file" is the name of the physical device that the file system will reside on. "Blocks" is the size of the file system in blocks. This command sets up the following structures needed for the operation of a file system:

1. A superblock
2. Inodes

Table 5.1   RP07 Sections

Section Number	Start Cylinder Number	End Cylinder Number	Length (1,000's of Blocks)
0	0	39	64
1	40	629	944
2	105	629	840
3	210	629	672
4	315	629	504
5	420	629	336
6	525	629	168
7	0	629	1,008

3. A free list

For example, we might want to make a full drive file system on an RP07 drive. We would issue the command:

/etc/mkfs   /dev/rdsk/1rp0707   1008000

The file system is created in section 7 of RP07 drive 0 on controller 1. The file system would have 1,008,000 blocks.

The special file is specified as CDNS (C = controller number, D = disk drive type, N = disk drive number, and S = section number). In this case C is 1, D is rpo7, N is 0, and S is 7.

The second part of making a file system is labeling it with its file system name and the disk pack name by using the /etc/labelit command. The simplified syntax for the /etc/labelit command is:

/etc/labelit   special_file   [filesysname   volume]

FILE SYSTEM ADMINISTRATION

"Special_file" is the name of the physical device that the file system resides on. "Filesysname" is the name we are giving to the file system. "Volume" is the name that we are giving to the disk pack that holds the file system. Used without filesysname and volume arguments, /etc/labelit reports the file system mounted on the special file. When /etc/labelit is invoked with filesysname and volume arguments, these names are inserted into the appropriate fields of the superblock of the file system residing on the named special file.

For example, to name the file system created earlier in this section **mcc1** and to name the disk pack that it resides on **pack1**, we would execute the command:

/etc/labelit /dev/rdsk/1rp0707 mcc1 pack1

Recall that the special file referenced is section 7 of RP07 drive 0 on controller 1.

5.4 Mounting and Unmounting File Systems

File systems are logically removable and may be mounted (made known to users) or unmounted (made invisible to users) using the /etc/mount, and /etc/umount commands. When a file system is mounted, its superblock is read into memory and an entry is made in the /etc/mnttab table. The /etc/mnttab file contains the information needed for currently mounted file systems. The /etc/mnttab file is created by the execution of the /etc/setmnt command at system generation time. The initial creation of the table will be discussed in Chapter 11. The following information is contained in /etc/mnttab :

1. A pointer to the special file (physical device) containing the file system
2. A pointer to a buffer containing the superblock for the file system
3. A pointer to the inode table entry for the mount point

The mount point is a previously created directory under / that matches the file system name.

The syntax of the /etc/mount command is as follows:

/etc/mount   [special_file   directory   [-r]]

"Special_file" is the name of the block special file on which the file system resides. "Directory" is the name of an existing directory that matches the name of the file system to be mounted. The optional -r argument can be used to mount the file system as read only. When the /etc/mount command is used without arguments it reports the names of the currently mounted file systems.

The syntax of the /etc/umount command is:

/etc/umount   special_file

where "special_file" is the name of the physical device on which the file system is being mounted. For example, if we wanted to mount the file system **mcc1** we would issue the commands:

mkdir   **/mcc1**

mount   **/dev/rdsk/1rp0707**   **/mcc1**

If we want to unmount file system **mcc1** we would execute the command:

/etc/umount   /dev/rdsk/1rp0707

5.5 Sanity Checking

Early versions of UNIX required a good deal of skill on the part of the system administrator in order to maintain file system integrity. UNIX SYSTEM V has automated the file

FILE SYSTEM ADMINISTRATION 59

system sanity checking and repair jobs in a manner that allows an experienced operator to sanity check and repair file systems successfully. The command used to check and repair file systems is /etc/fsck. Simplified syntax of the command is:

/etc/fsck   filesys_name...

"Filesys_name" is the name of a file system to be checked and repaired. If no file system name is listed, /etc/fsck checks a default list of file systems in /etc/checklist.

All file systems should be sanity checked and repaired after a system crash. An operator usually performs this task. /etc/fsck is interactive and asks the operator for concurrence with its planned actions. The operator either types 'y' or 'n' to concur with or cancel each proposed file system adjustment. The operator can also default all responses to 'y' with the -y option.

Some of the things /etc/fsck checks for are that:

1. All blocks in the file system are either in the free list or a file
2. No block is claimed by more than one file or a file and the freelist
3. The size of each file is correct as noted in the inode
4. The inodes are in the correct format
5. The link count for each file is correct
6. The free list is formatted correctly

5.6 Backup

Data integrity is one of the most important goals of a computer center. Even though disks may experience head crashes and other hardware problems, it is unacceptable for more than a few day's work to be lost. In order to preserve data integrity in the face of disk drives that occasionally fail, duplicate copies of file systems must be made frequently. The value of a particular file system will determine how frequently it will be backed up, and that value is usually determined by the end user of the file system. The backup frequency usually ranges from daily to weekly. The typical backup methods used are:

1. Full file system (volume) copy to tape or disk
2. File level copy of changed files to tape or disk (often called incremental backup)

5.6.1 Full Volume Copy to Tape or Disk

A quick way to copy a file system is to use the */etc/volcopy* program to copy the whole contents of a file system to another disk drive (with a removable pack) or to a reel of magnetic tape. The disk pack or tape reel can then be stored as a backup of the file system.

The syntax of the */etc/volcopy* command is

>*/etc/volcopy* filesys_name from_special from_volume to_special to_volume

where "filesys_name" is the name of the file system to be copied, "from_special" is the physical device that is the source for the copy, "from_volname" is the source physical volume name, "to_special" is the physical device that will receive the copy, and "to_volume" is the receiving physical volume name. The copy may be made to a disk drive (e. g. **/dev/rdsk/1s4**) or a tape drive (e. g. **/dev/rmt/1m**).

5.6.2 Incremental Copy to Disk

The problem with */etc/volcopy* is that an entire file system must be copied at once. Another method, called incremental file backup, allows backup of only specific files. A *cpio* copy may be made of only the files that have changed in a given time period. For example:

>*find* /usr -mtime 1 | *cpio* -oc > **/bck/usr/day.1**

would do a *cpio* copy of the files in the **/usr** file system that have been changed in the past day.

5.6.3 File Restoral

A file can be restored from the above backup by changing directory to the place where the file or directory is to reside and executing the command:

find /bck/usr/day.1 -name file_name | *cpio* -p .

5.7 Maintaining File Systems

Even in normal operation, two things happen to reduce file system usefulness: They become full, and they become fragmented and thus have inefficient access. Naturally, no more files can be added to a full file system, and its usefulness is severely impaired. A fragmented file system slows down I/O and generally bogs down a system. This section discusses how to deal with full and fragmented file systems.

5.7.1 Dealing with Full File Systems

There are two ways to deal with full file systems: (a) buy more disk drives and add more file systems; and (b) remove unneeded files from existing file systems.

Hardware configuration issues are discussed in Chapter 10. This section will deal with getting rid of unneeded files.

User cooperation is required to get rid of unneeded files without disruption. Chapter 2 explained methods of communication such as MOTD, *news*, broadcast messages, and *mail*, that could be used to ask users to clean up unneeded files.

The first step in cleaning up a file system is the identification of unneeded files. An appropriate *find* command can be used to identify the presence of **a.out, core, dead.letter,** and **ed.hup** files in a file system. Some computer centers have shell scripts that are run periodically and that inform users how much space they are wasting. These scripts send mail to the users asking them to clean up the files, or they may even automatically remove the files.

Table 5.2   Selected Dcopy Arguments

-sX	X=type of disk drive(4=RP06)
-an	Place n day old files after the free list.
-ffsize[:isize]	fsize=file system size; isize=number of inodes

5.7.2 Dealing with Fragmented File Systems

Input/output operations in a file system are at maximum efficiency immediately after the *mkfs* command has been properly executed to create the file system. As a file system ages, little used files may occupy the best areas of a disk drive, and the constant flow of data blocks in and out of the file system's free list may result in files that are inefficiently constructed. For example, an inefficiently created file might be one that had a small number of data blocks on each of a number of tracks, thus requiring several repositioning movements of the disk read/write head to access the file. *Dcopy* reorganizes the file system, puts the most used files in the optimum areas of disk, and brings the data blocks of files and the free list into efficiently accessed groups. In addition, *dcopy* can be used to change the number of inodes and/or blocks in the file system. *Dcopy* is used on an unmounted file system during system test time.

The simplified syntax of *dcopy* is:

/etc/dcopy   [-sX]   [-an]   [-ffsize[isize]]   in_fs   out_fs

where the use of the arguments is listed in Table 5.2.

The "-sX" argument specifies the type of disk drive(X) holding the file system and allows optimization of the rotational gap. The "-an" argument causes files more than n days old to be placed after the free list. The "-ffsize:[isize]" arguments allow specification of a different file system size and number of inodes than that in the original file system. "In_fs" is the name of the input file system and "out_fs" is the name of the output file system.

5.8 Summary

The UNIX operating system introduced the powerful concepts of the hierarchical file system and automated disk file allocation. In UNIX, files are organized in a treelike structure, and users can group files together that relate to a given task.

A disk drive can contain one or more UNIX file systems. Each file system has a control block called a superblock that is used to keep track of available disk resources for setting up file control blocks (called inodes) and file data.

An inode is the control structure that UNIX uses to keep track of a file. Data on the type of file, ownership, size, location of the file data, and time of last access and change are kept in the inode.

An administrator needs to have knowledge of the physical organization of the disk hardware being used in order to set up file systems. The administrator can then set up file systems with the *mkfs* and *labelit* commands.

The *mount* command makes a file system visible to users, and the *umount* command makes a file system invisible to users.

File systems are checked after a system crash with the *fsck* command, which repairs many common file system problems.

The *find* command can be used in conjunction with the *cpio* command to create a backup copy of recently changed files and to restore files on request from users.

System administrators can use the *dcopy* command to reorganize file systems that become fragmented. Administrators also can police file systems to get users to remove unneeded files. File systems that are allowed to become fragmented or nearly full have slow access.

5.9 Exercises

1. Where are each of the following pieces of information about a file stored?

a. Name
   b. Size
   c. Owner
   d. Permissions
   e. Inumber
2. What is the impact of automated file allocation and deallocation in the following areas?
   a. Training new users
   b. Efficiency and effectiveness of applications programmers
   c. Efficiency and effectiveness of system administrators
3. What command do you use to achieve each of the following goals?
   a. Initial setup of the file system
   b. Labeling the file system with its name and the disk pack name
   c. Making the file system visible to users
   d. Restoring optimum file system efficiency
4. Write a command to make a file system 1,008,000 blocks long on RP07 disk drive 1 on controller 0.
5. Write a command to label the above file system a1 and the pack it resides on pack2.
6. Write commands to mount the above file system.
7. Write a command to check the above file system.
8. Write a command to unmount the above file system.
9. Write a shell program to report the number of core files in a file system.
10. Write a shell program to report the number of files under a directory that have not been accessed in 6 months.
11. Discuss the potential problems associated with an emergency shutdown in which the in memory superblock

information is not copied to disk.

12. Discuss the advantages and disadvantages of incremental versus full volume backup.

6. PROCESS ADMINISTRATION

OBJECTIVES

After reading this chapter, you should be able to:

1. Explain the concept of a process.
2. Understand what foreground and background processes are.
3. Know what a signal is and be able to name the commonly used signals.
4. Control the response of processes to commonly used signals.
5. Obtain information on the processes in a system.
6. Determine if a process is degrading system operation.
7. Know how to terminate a process.

Processes are another important resource on a computer system and, in a real sense, do the work that the user wants done. Under normal conditions a system administrator pays little attention to processes, but when a UNIX system has a performance problem the administrator takes an active role in monitoring and controlling processes.

6.1 What a Process Is

A process is an instance of a running program. It includes a machine language (object) program, or a shell command *plus* additional information as to the current state of execution of the object program or shell command. The additional information includes: (a) the state of the registers, (b) the state of the stack, and (c) the state of the environment (that is, current values of shell variables).

All the above information must be kept because of the inherent nature of processes in a time sharing computer system.

In a traditional time sharing system we have one central processing unit but many, say N, processes. What this means is that each process in turn gets full use of the cpu for 1/N fraction of the time. Actual implementations get more complicated, but our goal is simply to understand that a time sharing system must continually stop processes, remember their state, and later restart them where they left off.

6.2 How Processes Are Created

If we ignore 'C' programmers for a moment, processes are created in the following ways:

1. The operating system establishes a shell process for each user who is currently logged on (explained in Chapter 4).

2. A user may create an additional process by typing the name of a command (for example, *pwd*). This process executes in the foreground, and the user must wait for its completion before regaining use of the keyboard.

3. A user may create additional processes by typing the name of a command followed by an '&.' For example:

    nroff -mm hugememo >hugememo.p&

    The user regains use of the keyboard immediately but could initiate many processes and potentially overload the system in this manner. A process created in this manner is called a background process.

4. A user may initiate several processes by typing a series of commands joined with pipes. For example:

    who | *wc* -l

    The *who* command would be one process and the *wc* command would be a second process.

Readers wanting to know more about processes are referred to *Operating System Design*, by Douglas Comer (Prentice-Hall, Englewood Cliffs, NJ, 1984).

6.3 Signals

We will first discuss what a signal is and then examine ways of controlling the effect of a signal on a process.

6.3.1 What a Signal Is

A signal is a piece of information sent to a process that has the potential to terminate the execution of the process. The most common signals are listed in Table 6.1. In general, a signal is passed to all processes that were started from a user's terminal. The shell exit signal is sent to all processes spawned by a user's shell process when the shell process dies. The hangup signal is sent when the data terminal ready lead drops on the user's data communications port. This is triggered when the dataset on a dial up port loses carrier or a terminal on a hardwired port is turned off. The interrupt signal is sent when the user depresses the delete key on the keyboard. The quit signal is sent when a user depresses the control and backslash keys on the keyboard. The kill signal is issued when the user executes a *kill* command with a -9 argument. The terminate signal is issued when the user executes a *kill* command. Only the kill signal is sure to kill a process.

6.3.2 Controlling Process Response to a Signal

Users have three options regarding how their processes treat signals:

1. Accept the default system action (usually termination of process execution)
2. Ignore the signal (except for the kill signal)
3. Specify the action they want taken

If you make no attempt to control signals, you get the default system action. If you want to ignore signals or provide a customized response to them, you can issue a *trap* command, which is built into *sh*. The syntax of the *trap* command is:

    trap ´command_list´ signal_list

Table 6.1 Selected Signals

Signal	How Generated	Signal Number
shell exit	shell process terminated	0–
hangup	DTR lead on port goes low	1
interrupt	delete key	2
quit	<control><backslash>	3
kill	kill -9 command	9
terminate	kill command	15

"Command list" is a list of UNIX commands and "signal_list" is a list of signal numbers from Table 6.1. The *trap* command is placed in the program that we want to trap signals for. For example, to have a process do nothing about (ignore) the hangup and interrupt signals, the following command is issued:

trap ″ 1 3

An example in which a process takes a customized action in response to a signal is:

trap ′ *rm* temp1; *exit* 1′ 1

This causes the process to remove a temporary file and return an unsatisfactory error code (1) upon receipt of a hangup signal.

6.4 Monitoring Processes

We shall describe the process monitoring appropriate for an ordinary user and system administrator. Then we shall discuss the varied types of information available on processes and methods of limiting the report on processes to only those processes of interest. The *ps* command is used to print information about processes.

6.4.1 Process Monitoring by Ordinary Users

Users may use the *ps* command without arguments to find out information about the processes they are running. Table 6.2 shows the result of running *ps* without arguments. The four columns shown in Table 6.2 are process ID (PID), the associated terminal that started the process (TTY), the cumulative execution time for the process (TIME), and the command that initiated the process (COMMAND). In Table 6.2 the user has three processes running: (a) a shell, (b) a *ps* command, and (c) an *nroff* command. Cumulative execution time is shown in the format M:SS, so that for *nroff* 0:15 means the execution time is 0 minutes and 15 seconds. If the execution time is less than 1 second, 0:00 is shown. The PID is needed should the user want to terminate the process.

6.4.2 Process Monitoring by System Administrators

On a stable, responsive system a system administrator pays little attention to processes. When system response time deteriorates, an administrator investigates the reason for slow response.

The administrator is concerned with *all* processes in a system and thus uses *ps* with the -e option to get a complete report of *all* processes in the system. The format is as shown in Table 6.2, but the report is many times longer. The administrator should look carefully at the TIME column and be alert to processes that have consumed one or more minutes of cpu time. The administrator uses the process information to search for the following situations:

1. A "runaway" process, that is an object program or shell with an infinite loop
2. A "wild" recursive process, one that calls itself endlessly
3. Inconsiderate users, such as people who run large jobs on a heavily loaded minicomputer on prime shift
4. The situation where normal computing load exceeds hardware capacity

The system administrator kills "runaway" processes, kills the

Table 6.2   Process Status Report

PID	TTY	TIME	COMMAND
2932	75	0:00	sh
25	75	0:00	ps
273	75	0:15	nroff

parent of a recursive process chain, tries to move large jobs off prime shift, and recommends the purchase of new hardware when existing hardware is overloaded in normal use. The system administrator can set a system parameter to limit the number of processes that an ordinary user can have.

6.4.3 Kinds of Data Available on Processes

The *ps* command without arguments provides basic information on processes. The -f (full listing) and -l (long listing) arguments to *ps* provide additional information. Table 6.3 shows the information displayed by *ps* when there is no argument, the -f argument, and the -l argument.

The *ps* manual page contains complete information on each field displayed by *ps*.

1. The F field (process flag) tells where the process is physically. This may be in memory, in the swap area, or in transit.
2. The S field (process state) tells the logical operating system state of the process, for example, sleeping, waiting, or running.
3. UID is the user ID.
4. PID is the process ID.
5. PPID is the parent process ID.
6. C is used for scheduling the processor.
7. PRI is the priority of the process – a high number means a low priority.

Table 6.3   Process Information

Heading	Description	When Printed
F	process flag	l
S	process state	l
UID	user ID	f or l
PID	process ID	always
PPID	parent process ID	f or l
C	processor scheduling	f or l
PRI	priority	l
NI	nice value	l
ADDR	address	l
SZ	process size	l
WCHAN	event waited for	l
STIME	process starting time	f
TTY	originating terminal	always
TIME	execution time	always
CMD	command name	always

8. NI is the nice value and is used in priority computation.

9. ADDR is the memory address for an in-memory process. It is the disk address for a process that is not in memory.

10. SZ is the process size in blocks.

11. WCHAN is the event on which the process is waiting. A null WCHAN field indicates the process is running.

12. STIME is the starting time for the process.

13. TTY is the terminal associated with the process.

14. TIME is the cumulative execution time for the process.

15. CMD is the name of the command that started the process.

6.4.4 Selecting a Subset of Processes

Ps has arguments that allow considerable flexibility in selecting the subset of processes to be reported on. Table 6.4 shows the

PROCESS ADMINISTRATION

Table 6.4 Selecting the Processes to Be Reported on

Argument	Processes Selected
none	only your processes
-e	every process
-a	every process except process group leaders
-p proclist	the processes whose PIDs are listed
-u uidlist	the processes whose UIDs are listed

arguments that determine the subset of processes reported on. Only the processes on your terminal will be reported on if no argument is provided to *ps*. The -e argument causes *ps* to report on every process. The -a argument causes *ps* to report on all processes except process leaders and background processes. The -p argument allows you to limit the report to a comma separated list of PIDs. The -u argument allows you to limit the report to a comma separated list of UIDs.

ps -u 25,103

reports only on the processes with a UID of 25 or 103.

6.5 Killing Processes

If a user backgrounds a process with an infinite loop, it would be up to the system administrator to kill it. This would be particularly true if the process was degrading system operation. The *kill* command is used to terminate a process. The syntax of the *kill* command is:

kill <signal_number> PID...

The administrator would use the *ps* command to get the PID. A process that could not be killed with a *kill* command would be killed with a *kill -9* command.

For example, suppose the system administrator used *ps* to determine that the process with PID 25634 was using a large amount of cpu time (minutes) and appeared to be running wild. System administrators might confirm their suspicion with a phone call to the user and then issue the following command to terminate the process.

   kill   25634

If *ps* showed that the process was still active,

   kill   -9   25634

would be used.

6.6 Summary

A process is a machine language program, together with associated user data and system data. A user can have only one foreground process, since the foreground process outputs to the user's terminal screen and inputs from the user's terminal keyboard. Users can have as many background processes as they wish, however. Background processes are created by typing a command name followed by an '&.'

A signal is a piece of information sent to a process by the operating system. Some commonly occurring signals mark the hangup of the user's terminal line, the depression of the delete key on the user's terminal keyboard, or issuance of a *kill* command. Users can control their processes' response to signals by including appropriate *trap* commands in their programs.

The *ps* command is used to obtain information on processes. Used without arguments the *ps* command prints only the process ID, the terminal associated with the process, the cumulative execution time, and the name of the command for the user who issued the command.

PROCESS ADMINISTRATION 75

Using the output of a *ps* -e command, the system administrator can spot "wild" recursive processes by numerous instances of a single command name, and an infinitely looping process by a large execution time.

The system administrator can kill a process with the *kill* command; if a process does not die with the *kill* command, a *kill* -9 command is used.

6.7 Exercises

1. Describe what a process is.
2. Can a user have more than one foreground process? Can a user have more than one background process?
3. What signal is sent to your processes when you hang up your phone line on a dial up port?
4. What signal is sent to your processes when you hit the delete key on your terminal keyboard?
5. What signal is sent to your processes when your shell process dies?
6. What signal is the only one guaranteed to kill a process?
7. How would you obtain information on processes belonging to the following?
    a. You
    b. Everyone
    c. Users with UIDs 15, 26, and 40
8. How can you tell if a process may be degrading system operation?
9. What options would you use with the *ps* command to get the following information on your processes?
    a. Cumulative execution time
    b. Priority
    c. Start time
    d. State

10. Write a command to terminate a process with PID 25743.

11. How can you differentiate between a normal process, a process with an infinite loop, and a "wild" recursive process?

7. OPERATIONS ADMINISTRATION

OBJECTIVES

After reading this chapter, you should be able to:

1. Describe the various elements of an operational schedule.
2. Design an operational schedule.
3. Execute commands on a set schedule.
4. List the major actions of a startup procedure.
5. List the major actions of a shutdown procedure.
6. Ready a file system for full volume backup.
7. Explain when incremental backups are appropriate.
8. Design a backup strategy.
9. Name some types of emergencies that affect computer systems.
10. Know how to avoid and deal with emergencies.
11. Describe the education and skills needed by a UNIX computer operator.

A system administrator negotiates the operational schedule of a UNIX system with end users, provides tools to implement the operational schedule, and helps to train operators.

7.1 Designing an Operational Schedule

Administrators and operators view time as divided into two parts: (a) prime shift, and (b) off prime shift.

7.1.1 Prime Shift

Prime shift is the time when a substantial number of end users are scheduled to work. Computer system availability must be kept at a high level (98–99 percent) during prime shift. System response is expected to be fast during this time also. A rough approximation of prime shift would be 7 A. M. to 6 P. M. Monday through Friday, at a typical installation.

Generally, system administrators and operators are expected to avoid making system changes or generating heavy system load during prime shift.

7.1.2 Off Prime Shift

Off prime shift is late evenings, nights, weekends, and holidays. It is the time when operators, administrators, and computer technicians perform file backups, preventive maintenance, and hardware and software upgrades. The amount of time needed to accomplish these tasks varies from one computer center to another and also with the passage of time within a given computer center. We will examine each of these activities and the factors that affect the required time to do them.

File Backup

Full volume and incremental backup are the two file backup methods. Because incremental backup does not necessarily require that the computer be made unavailable to users, it does not have a major impact on a computer's operational schedule. On the other hand, when full volume backup is used, the system must be made unavailable to users while the copies are being made and therefore has a major impact on an operational schedule.

The system administrator determines the frequency of file backup after consultation with users to determine their needs. Many computer centers make a full backup copy of each file system on at least a weekly basis and an incremental backup copy each night of the files that changed during the day.

For full volume copies, the file systems are unmounted at the time the copy is made to be sure that they do not change during the copy. The amount of time needed for full volume backup can be computed as follows:

1. Select one of your large file systems and *volcopy* it to tape during a period of low system use. Record the amount of time required for the copy.
2. Count the number of file systems that you have.
3. Multiply the copy time by the number of file systems and divide the product by the number of working tape drives.
4. Multiply the answer in the previous step by 1.5 to allow for the fact that an operator may not be immediately available as each tape is done.

For example, consider a computer center that has 40 file systems that took one-half hour each to copy to tape. The computer center has two tape drives. The amount of file backup time is computed as follows:

$$T = 1.5 \times (40 \times .50 \text{ hr.}) / 2 = 15 \text{ hr.}$$

Preventive Maintenance
Each hardware vendor recommends a schedule of preventive maintenance for its equipment. In particular, disk drives and tape drives need to be serviced periodically. A preventive maintenance schedule should be set up with each hardware vendor and sufficient time allowed for the necessary work. The amount of time needed for preventive maintenance depends on the amount and type of computer hardware in the center.

Hardware Upgrade
The computer hardware area is changing so rapidly that hardware upgrades are commonplace. The normal weekly operational schedule should allow sufficient time so that new tape drives, disk drives, a cpu upgrade, or a memory upgrade can be installed. The amount of time required for upgrading existing hardware or installing new hardware depends on the type and amount of hardware involved and can be determined by consultation with the vendor's computer engineer.

Software Upgrade
New versions of an operating system are released periodically. Bug fixes to an operating system and its utilities arrive more

often than complete releases. Time must be available to test system software changes. The amount of time required for software upgrade depends on the frequency of new software releases and bug fixes and is determined by consultation with the vendor's marketing support personnel.

7.1.3 Operational Schedule Example

Table 7.1 shows a possible operational schedule for a UNIX computer center. File backup requires eight hours and is done in two four-hour parts early on Wednesday and Friday mornings. System test time starts at 9 P. M. (21:00) Tuesday and Thursday night and extends for eight hours each evening. The system test periods are used only when needed; otherwise the system is available.

7.2 Implementing an Operational Schedule

Three major operational events are startup, shutdown, and file backup.

7.2.1 Startup

The two parts of a startup procedure are coming up in single-user mode and making a transition to multi-user mode.

Single-User Mode

In single-user mode, only the system console is active; in multi-user mode, the system console plus the multiplexer ports are active. A system is powered up according to hardware vendor instructions and then "bootstraped" into UNIX single-user mode. Each specific hardware configuration has a primitive "bootstrap," or boot program. In most modern computers the primitive boot sequence initiation is usually as simple as turning on the cpu power switch, pressing a button, or keying a specific character sequence into the system console. Refer to the vendor's manual for your system to determine the proper boot procedure. The UNIX PC boots when power is turned on. The boot procedure for the 3B20 computer is specified on the boot(8) manual page of the *UNIX System V Release 2.0 Administrator Reference Manual*.

The primitive bootstrap program on a minicomputer requests a disk drive number from the operator. The disk boot program is read in from block 0 of the disk drive specified. The disk boot program of a minicomputer requests the path

Table 7.1   Operational Schedule Example

Day	Available	System Test	File Backup
Monday	0:00 — 24:00		
Tuesday	0:00 — 21:00	21:00 - 5:00 (W)	
Wednesday	5:00 — 24:00		0:00 — 4:00
Thursday	0:00 — 21:00	21:00 — 5:00 (F)	
Friday	5:00 — 24:00		0:00 — 4:00
Saturday	0:00 — 24:00		
Sunday	0:00 — 24:00		

name of the UNIX that is to be started. When the operator enters the path name of the UNIX instance to be started, that file is executed and the system is then running UNIX in single-user mode.

Preparation for Transition to Multi-User Mode
Before a system is brought up to multi-user mode, all the file systems must be checked with *fsck*. A complete set of file systems to be checked should be placed in /etc/checklist, and from then on the operator can initiate the checking of all file systems simply by typing *fsck*. The file system check program is interactive, and the operator should normally be present to confirm or deny the file system adjustments proposed by *fsck*. The -y option can be used on *fsck* to avoid the need for operator intervention. *Fsck* is used after a crash and whenever problems are suspected; a system is not brought up in multi-user mode until all file systems are clean.

Transition to Multi-User Mode
The first step in making the transition to multi-user mode is setting the date. The date is set with the *date* command. The syntax of the *date* command is as follows:

    date   mmddhhmmyy

where the leftmost "mm" is month, "dd" is day, "hh" is hour, "mm" is minute, and "yy" is year. For example:

$ *date* 1030013085

sets the date to October 30, 1985, 1:30 A. M. The system operates on GMT, and the *date* program automatically converts to and from local time. Note that the date should only be set when the system is in single-user mode.

A shell called /etc/rc is then executed. The shell executes /etc/mount commands for all user file systems. The shell then turns on the multiplexer ports by executing the command:

$ *init* 2

It is assumed that /etc/inittab has been set up to properly define all the ports on the system (see Chapter 4 for how to do this). The shell may perform other installation-dependent actions based on local needs.

7.2.2 Shutdown

A system may go from multi-user mode to single-user mode on approximately a weekly basis for file saves. It is much less common for a system to be shut down "hard," that is, powered down.

Transition from Multi-User Mode to Single-User Mode

The /etc/shutdown command is used to bring a system from multi-user mode to single-user mode. It does the following:

1. Warns users to save their files and log off
2. Kills all user processes
3. Unmounts all file systems
4. Updates the disk super blocks from fast memory

Hard Shutdown

A "hard" shutdown, when the system is powered down, is rarely necessary. A hard shutdown takes place, for example, if the system is to be moved, if major equipment reconfiguration is to take place, or if a major lightning storm (with accompanying fluctuating power) is expected. While power conditioning and battery backup can eliminate the need for shutdown during a major lightning storm, it can be expensive. A hard shutdown involves powering down the disk drives, cpu, and other peripheral equipment.

7.2.3 File Backup

Bringing the file systems to a state of quiescence in preparation for file backup will be discussed followed by information on choosing a backup strategy.

Making a File System Quiescent

If several file systems are to be backed up, the transition from multi-user to single-user mode should be executed and then the file backups done. The purpose of doing this is to make the file systems quiescent so that a valid "snapshot" of the file systems can be made on tape or disk.

It is possible to manually bring one file system to a quiescent state by asking users not to access it, killing the shells of the offenders, and unmounting the file system. This procedure is very time-consuming and is seldom used.

Choosing a Backup Methodology

Choices must be made regarding frequency of backup and type of backup (full-volume copy or incremental file copy). Weekly full-volume backups are common in many UNIX computer centers. The labor-intensive nature of the disk-to-tape copy and the requirement for the file systems to be brought to a state of quiescence makes daily full-volume backup impractical.

Incremental file backup provides a means to fill in the gap between weekly full-volume backups. Incremental file backup involves copying only the files that have changed in the last day (or other time period decided by the administrator). Changed files can be found with the following command:

```
$ find   file_sys_name   -mtime 1   -print  \;
```

The *find* command provides a list of pathnames of files and directories that were changed within the past day. The list of file names generated by the above command is piped to the *cpio* command and the resulting incremental backup file is stored on a different disk drive than the one with the original copy of the files. In this fashion, work will not be lost unless both these disk drives crash.

Restoring a File

Restoring a file is facilitated by keeping the incremental backup files on line. Each night's incremental backup file is kept in a separate directory. The number of night's backups that would be kept on line is determined by the amount of disk space available for this purpose.

Let's take a look at restoring a file named 'lost' that was created during prime shift on Monday, backed up on Monday night, and inadvertently destroyed by its owner on Tuesday morning. We assume that the Monday night incremental backup file is on line in directory **/monib**. The following procedure is used:

1. *cd* to the user directory where the file is to be restored
2. $ find . -name lost | cpio -p .

7.2.4 Using Cron

Cron is a clock demon that executes commands from **/usr/spool/cron/crontabs** at specified times. It is useful in triggering incremental file backups and other administrative work at times of low system load and even when the system is unattended. A **crontab** entry consists of six fields. The first five fields specify when the command is to be run, and the sixth field is the command. The time specification fields from left to right are: minute of the hour (0−59), hour of the day (0−23), day of the month, month, and day of the week (Monday = 1, Sunday = 7). Each time specification field can contain an integer constant or '*', which is a wild card.

For example, to execute the system incremental backup shell, *ibshell*, at 1:15 A. M. each morning the following entry is made:

15 1 * * * *ibshell*

To execute the system billing shell, *billing*, at 2:30 P. M. on the first of each month, the following entry is made:

30 2 1 * * *billing*

7.3 Handling Emergencies

Emergencies can occur at any time. Two kinds of emergencies will be considered: system crash and disaster. Many computer centers find it useful to provide either a 24-hour telephone answering service or operational and administrative personnel with "beepers" to facilitate response to emergencies whenever they occur. If users have a major problem when a system is unattended, they can call the answering-service or beeper number to report the problem.

7.3.1 Crash

A "crash" means the system stops running. The first step in dealing with a crash is to take a dump of UNIX. Use the *dump* command to take a dump. Use the *crash* command after the fact to analyze the dump. In a crash situation, the best thing for a beginning system administrator to do is to call for help from an experienced system administrator. If an experienced system administrator is not available, take a dump and try a reboot. If the problem continues and the hardware is suspected, a hardware vendor customer engineer should be called in to check the hardware.

7.3.2 Dealing with Disaster

A disaster would be a fire or storm or some other occurrence. The best way to handle a disaster is to avoid it. You can get information on disaster preparedness from your local technical library or computer vendor. Some suggestions are:

1. Install smoke and water detectors

2. Install a nondestructive fire suppression system
3. Have duplicate power feeds to the computer room
4. Limit access to the computer room to authorized personnel
5. Keep a copy of backup tapes at another site
6. Keep a copy of the specification of your hardware configuration at another site
7. Have a person be responsible for knowing where surplus space and equipment is located

7.4 Operator Training

A computer operator needs both fundamental knowledge of computer science and specific skills. Requirements in each of these areas will be discussed. In a large computer center, the operations supervisor ensures that operators are properly trained; in a small computer center, a system administrator may be responsible for operator training.

7.4.1 Basic Knowledge

Traditional courses in Introduction to Computer Science and Data Structures along with a UNIX shell programming course provide a good basis for UNIX operations. The shell course would be taught on a UNIX system and should give the student a knowledge of at least one UNIX editor (preferably a screen editor for reasons of efficiency). These three courses provide the conceptual framework needed for UNIX operations. Virtually all colleges offer Introduction to Computer Science and Data Structures courses. The UNIX shell programming course is available only when a local college has access to a UNIX system. Fortunately, vendors may offer a UNIX shell course compressed into a one-week schedule at a customer site. This type of course is expensive, however, with a characteristic price of around $750 per student.

7.4.2 Specific Skills

Some skills are difficult to teach in a classroom environment. For example, most colleges that have a UNIX system have only one console and one tape drive, thus making it impractical to teach console-dependent operations or operation of a tape drive to a large number of students. Operators should develop abilities to do the following:

1. Boot the system
2. Bring the system to multi-user mode
3. Shut down the system
4. Read a tape
5. Mount and unmount a disk pack
6. Add and delete logins
7. Use the installation's file back-up shell
8. Run the local area network
9. Restart demons (programs that run periodically)

7.5 Summary

An operational schedule consists of prime shift, when the end users' work is done, and off prime shift. System test time is scheduled during off prime shift. File backups also take place during off prime shift. Prime shift is determined by the users' work schedule. The duration and scheduling of system test time depends on the type and amount of equipment in the computer configuration and other user requirements. File backup time depends on the amount of disk to be backed up, available equipment for backup, and user requirements.

A minicomputer system is started up with a ROM bootstrap program that brings in a larger boot program from a disk drive specified at the console. The disk boot program brings up UNIX in single-user mode. After the file systems have been checked and mounted, the *init* program is executed to spawn the processes needed in multi-user mode. Typically, the steps after booting are automated in an installation *startup* shell.

A minicomputer system is brought from multi-user to single-user mode by warning users to log off, killing all terminal processes, and unmounting user file systems. Typically, the steps are automated in an installation *shutdown* shell.

File backup ensures that the probability of losing a substantial amount of user work is small. File backup may involve copying a whole file system to a disk drive or tape drive; an alternative is to copy only files that have changed recently to a disk drive.

Commands are executed on an unattended system by making an entry in the **crontab** file, consisting of six fields. The first five fields specify when the command will be run, and the sixth field is the actual command to run. The ability to schedule the automatic execution of commands in advance is a significant operational advantage of UNIX.

It is necessary to be prepared for emergencies such as system crashes and physical damage. A crash is dealt with by taking a dump and analyzing it. Other emergencies are dealt with by installing procedures and equipment that physically protect the computer system and facilitate its prompt replication, should it be destroyed.

A UNIX system administrator may be responsible for training UNIX operators. Operators need basic education in computer science concepts, including courses in introduction to computer science, data structures, and shell; they also need specific skills such as running the system startup, shut-down, and backup programs.

7.6 Exercises

1. Design an operational schedule for a research and development facility that has a 9:00 A. M. to 5:00 P. M. work schedule. Assume weekly file backup to tape takes 4 hours.

2. Design an operational schedule for a shopping center that is open from 10:00 A. M. to 10:00 P. M. every day of the week. Assume weekly file backup to tape takes 6 hours.

3. Describe how to boot a UNIX PC; a 3B20.

4. What actions are taken to prepare to go from single-user to multi-user mode?

5. What actions are taken to go from multi-user to single-user mode?

OPERATIONS ADMINISTRATION

6. Can you properly *volcopy* a live file system?
7. Can you do an incremental backup of a live file system? What conditions should be met before this is attempted?
8. What is the difference between full volume copies and incremental file copies?
9. Describe how you would execute a command on an unattended system.
10. What would you do if a UNIX system crashed?
11. What basic computer science knowledge should an operator have? What skills should a computer center train an operator in?

8. SECURITY ADMINISTRATION

OBJECTIVES

After reading this chapter, you should be able to:

1. Handle file and directory modes appropriately.
2. Use groups to limit file access.
3. Encrypt files.
4. Detect and eliminate unauthorized superusers.
5. Effectively control logins.
6. Implement effective password security.
7. Effectively limit telecommunications access to a system.
8. Limit tape production.
9. Set up and maintain the physical security of the computer room.

A secure system should allow system use and file access only by authorized users. No one should be allowed to deny use of the system to authorized users.

Computer centers have varied goals in the security area. All centers are concerned that authorized users are not denied access to the system. Most are concerned that only authorized users are able to use the system. Some want file access closely controlled for some or all groups of users, and others may be unconcerned about this issue. Good system administrators are able to run their systems as securely as their management decides is necessary.

8.1 Handling File and Directory Modes

The basic means of protecting your programs and data on a UNIX system is by having the mode set properly on each file and directory. UNIX allows you to specify read, write, and execute permissions for three classes of user: (a) yourself, (b) your group, and (c) others.

Since "others" can be anyone, including an access from another UNIX system, it is important not to allow write access by "other." Generally, you should give yourself read, write, and execute permission on a directory and read and write permission on a file. Also, you usually should allow members of your group read and execute (search) permission on a directory and read permission on a file. Unless there is some important reason to do otherwise, all permissions are usually denied to others.

8.1.1 Setting UMASK in /etc/profile

Whenever a user creates a file using an editor or file movement command, the system sets default modes for the file using UMASK. The UMASK specifies what permissions to turn off (mask). The UMASK is specified as a 3-digit octal number. The format of the UMASK value is UGO. The digit in the U position specifies permissions to be denied for you, the owner of the file. The digit in the G position specifies permissions to be denied for your group. The digit in the O position specifies permissions to be denied for others. For example a UMASK of 037 would turn off write and execute permission for your group and turn off all permissions for others.

The format of the bit string specified by each octal digit in the UMASK is rwx. The r bit is read, the w bit is write and the x bit is execute or search. The 3 in 037 corresponds to the binary value 011. The 0 means don't turn off read permission. The 1 in the middle means turn off write permission. The 1 on the right means turn off execute permission.

You should set the UMASK in /etc/profile because the login program executes /etc/profile as it logs on each user. If the user has not set UMASK in his or her .profile, the UMASK in /etc/profile controls the default setting of file and directory modes. A UMASK of 037 is appropriate for a secure system. A UMASK of 077 is appropriate for an extremely secure system.

The above procedures relate to controlling the default permissions given to a file. Users can modify these permissions later using the *chmod* command. A system administrator can only try to assure that the initial permissions are appropriate from a security standpoint.

8.1.2 Using Groups

The use of groups can be a big help in implementing a secure system. Setting up appropriate groups and giving files and directories adequate group permissions can help to make a system both secure and easily used.

UNIX allows for group IDs. The administrator must map appropriate organizational groups (such as supervisory group or department) into UNIX groups. A group is normally set up for each project or community of interest.

Groups are implemented by making entries in the /etc/group file. The entries consist of four fields:

1. Group name
2. Password
3. Numeric group ID number
4. Login names in the group

For example consider:

proj1::23:ed,sally,mary

This entry defines a group named "proj1." The second, password, field is null, indicating that no password is required to change to this group. If a ',' is placed in this field, the first user is prompted to give a password, which is encrypted and installed in encrypted form, and subsequent users are required to provide the password before being given the group permission. The third field has a Group ID (GID) of 23. Logins ed, sally, and mary are listed as members of the group.

SECURITY ADMINISTRATION

CPU DESIGN DEPT.	OS DESIGN DEPT.	COMPILER DESIGN DEPT.
J. Cho, Supv.	A. Richards, Supv.	S. Levine, Supv.
J. Adams	E. Edwards	J. Blake
H. Garcia	F. Smith	K. Burke
P. Brady	J. Kovacs	D. Zbdiensky
K. Jones		

Figure 8.1 Organization Chart for the Venus Company

There are two ways to gain group privileges. The first is to have an /etc/passwd file entry that has the GID of the group. In this case you are given the group access privilege during login. The second way is to execute a *newgrp* command to enter the group. If a login is listed in the fourth field of the /etc/group entry for that group, the login will be allowed to change to the specified group. The command:

newgrp proj1

could be executed by logins ed, mary, or sally to change group to proj1 based on the above example of the /etc/group file.

8.1.3 An Example to Show Proper Use of Groups

Figure 8.1 shows a sample organization chart for the Venus Company. The Venus Company produces a new computer on a chip, complete with standard system software. The company has a department to design the hardware (CPU Design Department), a department to design the operating system (OS Design Department), and a department to design compilers (Compiler Design Department). The Venus Company is in a highly competitive market with high employee turnover; its management has decided to limit information to personnel having a "need to know."

/etc/passwd file for the Venus Company

jja:encryptedpassword:100:1000:j.j.adams(cho):/a1/gp1/ja:
heg:encryptedpassword:101:1000:h.e.garcia(cho):/a1/gp1/hg:
pjb:encryptedpassword:102:1000:p.j.brady(cho):/a1/gp1/pb:
kkj:encryptedpassword:103:1000:k.k.jones(cho):/a1/gp1/kj
ebe:encryptedpassword:104:2000:e.b.edwards(richards):/a1/gp2/ee:
fms:encryptedpassword:105:2000:f.m.smith(richards):/a1/gp2/fs:
jbk:encryptedpassword:106:2000:j.b.kovacs(richards):/a1/gp2/jk:
jrb:encryptedpassword:107:3000:j.r.blake(levine):/a1/gp3/jb:
kjb:encryptedpassword:108:3000:k.j.burke(levine):/a1/gp3/kb:
dlz:encryptedpassword:109:3000:d.l.zbdensky(levine):/a1/gp3/dz:

/etc/group file for the Venus Company

cpu::1000:ebe,fms,jbk
os::2000:
comp::3000:

Figure 8.2   Passwd and Group Files for the Venus Company

Figure 8.2 shows the /etc/passwd and /etc/group files for the Venus Company. Let's examine the /etc/passwd file first. Every member of the company has a unique user identification number (the third field). Note that the group identification number is the same for all members of a department. The name of the person responsible for each login is shown in the fifth, or comment, field for ease of reference. The sixth field shows the login directory, and the null seventh field indicates that each user gets a normal shell on login. This configuration of the /etc/passwd file makes sharing of information easy for the members of a department. All members of a department share a common group identification number. This allows department members to give privileges to fellow department members without exposing the files to others.

SECURITY ADMINISTRATION

Now we will examine the **/etc/group** file. One function this file serves is to define the group name associated with each group identification number (cpu is associated with 1000, for example). Another use of this file is to allow logins usually associated with one group to take on the group identification number of another group when desired. The members of the Operating System Department sometimes need access to the files and directories of the CPU Department. This need is taken care of by listing the login names of the Operating System Department members in the fourth field of the cpu group entry. In order to take on the privileges associated with the cpu group, members of the Operating System Department need only do a *newgrp* to the cpu group.

8.1.4 Automating Protection

Security measures should be automated. One good way to protect file systems is to set the permissions securely overnight using a shell executed by *cron*. On transition from single-user to multi-user state, the system executes a shell called */etc/rc*. In */etc/rc*, the mode of each file system should be set appropriately. Specifically, write by other permission should be removed.

Note that the mode change is done on a *filesystem* basis rather than a file by file basis. Turning off permissions for others on a filesystem or high-level directory gives good protection with a minimum of effort. One high-level directory without other permission is sufficient to secure everything beneath it.

8.2 Encrypting Files

Users should be advised that *especially* sensitive files should be encrypted using the *crypt* command. Only the person who knows the encryption key should be able to convert an encrypted file to clear text. Choose a key that is long and contains nonalphabetic characters to make the key more difficult to crack. The syntax of the *crypt* command is:

crypt key <clear >cryptic

An example of encrypting a file follows:

$*crypt* tawney1 <clearmemo >cryptmemo

$ *rm* clearmemo

Here is how to decrypt **cryptmemo**.

$*crypt* tawney1 <cryptmemo >clearmemo

The clear copy of the memo is now available in the file **clearmemo**. *Don't forget the password that you used for file encryption. If you do, you cannot access a readable copy of the file.*

8.3 Controlling Superusers

The superuser password should be divulged only to a small number of people, including the system operators and system administrators. Since a superuser can access any file and execute any command on a UNIX system, it is a privilege that should be given only to trustworthy personnel. A malevolent superuser has the capability of denying system access to everyone and destroying files. Some computer centers require superusers to sign an agreement that acknowledges the special trust and responsibility for ethical behavior in the exercise of superuser privileges.

The superuser password should be long and should contain nonalphabetic characters to make it more difficult to break. In addition, the superuser password should be changed at least monthly. Whenever a superuser leaves your computer center, the superuser password should be changed *IMMEDIATELY*. Particular care should be taken that the superuser password is not entered in a manner that allows an open view to unauthorized personnel.

An operator login should be set up to do routine tasks. Consoles should be left logged onto the operator login rather than the superuser login. A terminal left logged on a superuser should not be left unattended.

8.4 Managing Logins

A shell should be written and run periodically from the system **crontab** that generates a report containing all the login names for which a supervisor is responsible. Of course, for this strategy to work, all logins on the system must have a supervisor's name or initials in each password file entry. If supervisors read their login reports and report unneeded logins to the system administrator, the password file can be kept up to date. When an employee leaves the company, his or her supervisor should know to immediately ask a system administrator to remove the former employee's login. A useful backup mechanism would be to have the person responsible for deleting a person who left the company from the payroll system to also notify the system administrator to delete the person's login.

8.5 Enhancing Password Security

Several methods may be used to increase password security: password aging, long passwords, varied passwords, and random passwords.

8.5.1 Password Aging

The security of a system is enhanced by the frequent changing of passwords. An administrator can control the frequency with which users must change passwords by editing the password field of the **/etc/passwd** file. Forcing password expiration, also known as password aging, is triggered by putting a ',' after the password, followed by a character that specifies the maximum number of weeks that a password is valid. A second character is appended to specify the minimum number of weeks that must elapse before the password may be changed. The purpose of the minimum specification is to prevent the user from changing his or her password and then immediately changing it back to its initial value. The alphabet for setting the maximum and minimum periods is (. , /, 0−9, A−Z, a−z). The character '.' corresponds to 0 weeks and the character 'Z' corresponds to 38 weeks. Passwords should expire monthly at most and remain unchanged for at least a week. In order to implement this suggestion, the characters ',2/' are appended to the password fields in the /etc/passwd file.

8.5.2 Long Passwords

Passwords should have at least six characters. If you use the full ASCII character set (128 characters) in choosing your password, each additional character increases the difficulty of cracking the password by a factor of 128. The *passwd* command forces a password to have at least 6 characters in order to gain the advantage associated with a long password.

8.5.3 Varied Passwords

Use the whole character set when choosing characters for a password. If you choose your characters from a set containing 100 characters, you gain a factor of 10 in security compared with choosing characters from a set of 10 characters for each character in the password. For example, a 6-character password, where each character is chosen from the 100-character set, is 1,000,000 times harder to crack than a 6-character password where each character was chosen from the 10-character set. The *passwd* command forces a password to have at least two alphabetic characters and one numeric or special character to gain the advantage associated with a password chosen from a large character set.

8.5.4 Random Passwords

If you choose such passwords as your name, your spouse's name, or your children's name, they can be easily cracked by someone who knows you. Avoid using passwords that can easily be associated with you.

8.6 Limiting Telecommunications Access

You should take action to limit unauthorized use of your system. An unauthorized person should not be able to find out the phone number of your system and log on.

1. Don't publicize the phone number of your dial up ports outside your organization. Knowledge of a time sharing system's phone number is the first step to breaking into the system.

2. Make sure your login program drops the line after a small number of unsuccessful login attempts. Give the person or computer attempting penetration a challenge. The

SECURITY ADMINISTRATION

greater the average time per login attempt, the lower the probability of guessing a valid login name and password. Slow down the potential penetrator.

3. Log unsuccessful login attempts and have a shell report the number of unsuccessful login attempts on a periodic basis. When you see the unsuccessful login attempts increase dramatically, chances are good that attempted penetration is taking place.

4. Don't configure more dial up ports than you need. If the number of ports that you have is matched to your organization's needs, ports tied up in a penetration attempt will cause users to complain about lack of access, increasing the chance that the penetration attempt will be noticed.

5. *uucp* is a UNIX remote execution and file transfer command. It is traditional for UNIX sites to exchange *uucp* logins and passwords. Be very strict as to the list of commands that may be executed by *uucp*. You have no idea who is going to be accessing your system via *uucp*.

8.7 Limiting Tape Production

Tape is a good medium for reliably storing large quantities of information. Reels of tape are easily carried. For this reason you may need to limit access to the tape drives on your system. In many computer centers, ordinary users are allowed to make tapes. In some very secure computer centers, tape manufacturing is limited to operators.

If tapes are to be manufactured only by operators, users should fill out a written request for producing a tape and write a shell to produce the tape (see Figures 8.3 and 8.4). The operator then logs the request, executes the shell, and gives the user the tape. The shell is executed with the UID of the requester.

8.8 Computer Room Security

A locked door should limit access to the computer room. Traditional keys or magnetic cards may be used to control access.

```
DIR=/a1/pjb/comp
cd $DIR
find . -print | cpio -ocB >/dev/rmt8
echo "TAPE READY"
```

Figure 8.3   Sample Tape Production Shell

USER NAME _____

DATE _____

ROOM NUMBER _____

PHONE NUMBER _____

FULL PATH NAME OF TAPE PRODUCTION SHELL _____

OPERATOR INITIALS _____   DATE TAPE PRODUCED _____

NUMBER OF BLOCKS _____

REMARKS _____

Figure 8.4   Tape Production Request

Access to the computer room should be limited to persons who need to be there. Generally, the following personnel need access to the computer room:

1. Computer operators
2. System administrators
3. Computer and peripheral device installation and repair technicians
4. Software developers using special purpose peripheral devices

The room should be attended by an operator or administrator whenever outside technicians are working in the room. Computer consoles should not be left logged on with the "superuser" login. An operator login should be set up and the consoles left logged in with the operator login.

8.9 Summary

UMASK controls the mode with which files are created. The system administrator can influence file and directory security in a favorable manner by setting the UMASK shell variable in the **/etc/profile** file to a secure value. Since **/etc/profile** is executed as each user logs on, UMASK will be set securely. Users can undo this protection by resetting UMASK in their **.profile** file or by using *chmod*, but that will be their responsibility.

System administrators can learn the organization of the users of their system and establish groups so that members of a project can share files with each other but protect them from other users.

A system administrator can encourage users to use the *crypt* command to encrypt sensitive files. These files are then protected from everyone's view except perhaps an expert cryptologist with a large amount of computing power available.

Login management procedures should be set up to allow only authorized people to get logins. Users and their supervisors should have responsibility for logins. Logins of people leaving the organization should be promptly deleted.

Passwords should be used effectively on all logins. The password field of the **/etc/passwd** file should be set up to force users to change passwords monthly and to prevent them from immediately changing back to their old password. Users should be encouraged to avoid passwords that are easily discovered, such as a spouse's or a child's name.

Telecommunications access to the system should be controlled. The phone number of the system should not be published outside your organization. The system should be set up to drop a dial up line after a small number of unsuccessful login attempts; unsuccessful login attempts should be recorded.

Production of tapes should be limited to operators and a small number of users.

The computer room should be physically secured, with access limited to essential personnel. Consoles should not be left logged onto the "superuser" login.

8.10 Exercises

1. What would you set your UMASK to in your .profile if you wanted to deny write permission to members of your group and others?

2. Show the entry that you would make in the /etc/group file to define a group named csc246 that included logins mary, joe, and rick. Use a GID of 2000 in your answer.

3. What would be the effect of setting up two entries in the /etc/group file that had the same GID?

4. Give the command to encrypt file **file1** with key abc123.

5. Write a shell that accepts a supervisor's initials as an argument and prints all the entries in the /etc/passwd file relating to that supervisor.

6. What field of what file would you edit to specify the maximum and minimum periods for which a password is valid? What value would you insert to force passwords to be changed at least every 6 weeks and remain unchanged for at least 2 weeks?

7. If you allowed only the digits 0−9 in a password, on the average, how many tries would it take to break a 4 digit password?

8. Explain why it is important to keep a copy of backup tapes somewhere other than just in the computer room.

9. Write a shell to find all files with the superuser UID in the /a1 file system.

10. Discuss methods to limit telecommunications access to your system.

11. Discuss methods to provide physical security for your computer room.

9. ADMINISTRATION OF COMPUTING RESOURCES

OBJECTIVES

After reading this chapter, you should be able to:

1. State a philosophy for administering computing resources.
2. Monitor disk usage.
3. Monitor cpu usage.
4. Monitor port usage.
5. Identify and eliminate bottlenecks.
6. Solve computing resource problems.

A successful system administrator is one who provides sufficient computing resources for users to accomplish their goals on schedule and in an economical fashion.

9.1 Resource Administration Objectives

A reasonable objective for a system administrator might be to provide a level of service that satisfies the needs of the user community with a minimum of capital outlay and operating expense. Generally, a "smooth running system" is desirable. When users copy a file, they expect the copy to work rather than fail because of a lack of inodes or disk blocks. When users execute a text processing command, they expect results within a few seconds rather than having to wait several minutes as a result of an overloaded central processing unit. Likewise, when users attempt to log in they expect to get into the system and not have to make multiple attempts because all ports are busy.

If there are several computer systems in a computer center, it is normally expected that they provide a roughly comparable level of service. If a substantial difference exists, it should be the result of a conscious management decision.

9.2 Monitoring Free Space

First we shall discuss the use of a "block" as the unit of measure for disk free space. Then, the commands used for measuring disk free space will be explained.

9.2.1 What Size Block?

Originally, a block was a contiguous 512 byte area of disk with a unique address. As larger capacity disk drives became available, 1,024 and 4,096 byte blocks were sometimes used. Before becoming deeply involved in disk free space analysis, you should find out the block size used on your system, either by reading the documentation supplied with your software or by calling the vendor technical support person for your software.

9.2.2 The *df* Command

The *df* command is used to determine total free space for each file system. It will tell you how close you are to running out of disk space. The simplified syntax of the *df* command is:

df [-t] [file_sys_name...]

Df prints out the number of free blocks and inodes available in the named file systems. If no file system names are specified, information is printed on all mounted file systems. If the "-t" argument is used, the original file system size and number of inodes is also printed.

9.2.3 The *du* Command

The *du* command computes block usage in a subtree of a file system. It is useful in determining the number of blocks contained in a file or in and beneath a directory. It is often used with a user's login directory as an argument in order to determine that user's disk usage. The *du* command must be used from a login with "superuser" permissions in order to get accurate block counts. When *du* is used by nonsuperusers, it silently ignores files and directories that the user does not have permission to access.

The simplified syntax of the *du* command is:

    du   [-rs]   name...

Du computes and prints the number of blocks contained in the named directories and files. The default name is '.'. The "-s" argument causes only the grand total number of blocks to be printed for each name. Otherwise, a subtotal is printed for each subdirectory. The "-r" argument makes *du* report any directories or files skipped because of lack of access permission and should *always* be used when *du* is executed by a login without "superuser" permission.

9.3 Monitoring Cpu Usage

There are two aspects to monitoring cpu usage. The first is gathering process accounting data; the second is using the process accounting data.

9.3.1 Gathering Process Accounting Data

The UNIX operating system is capable of generating a process accounting record as each process terminates. This record is appended to a process accounting file.

We shall examine how to turn on process accounting, how to turn off process accounting, and the constituent fields of the process accounting record.

Turning Process Accounting On or Off

The accounting programs are in the **/usr/lib/acct** directory. This directory should be added to the administrator's PATH for ease of command execution. The *"turnacct* on" command turns process accounting on. The *"turnacct* off" command turns process accounting off.

Process accounting is normally turned on by the system *startup* shell and turned off by the system *shutdown* shell. *Turnacct* can only be used by a superuser.

Contents of the Process Accounting Record

The process accounting record for a process contains information that identifies the user and the resource usage by the process in terms of cpu cycles, memory, and input/output. The following fields are contained in the process accounting record: accounting flag, exit status, UID, tty, beginning time, user time (clock tics), system time (clock tics), elapsed time (clock tics), memory usage (clicks), characters transferred by read/write, blocks transferred by read/write, command name, accounting buffer address, and pointer to accounting file inode.

The accounting flag is used to record whether or not the process has executed the *fork* command. "Exit status" is the value returned when the process terminated. "UID" is the user ID of the process owner. "GID" is the group ID of the process owner. "Tty" is the name of the port that initiated the process. "Beginning time" is the time the process started executing.

"User time" is the amount of time the process was executing in user mode. This could be thought of as time spent executing user written code rather than system subprograms. This time is measured in clock tics, which is a hardware-dependent unit of time. For a 3B20 computer, a clock tic is 10 milliseconds.

"System time" is the amount of time the process spends executing system (section 2) subprograms and is measured in clock tics. "Elapsed time" is the amount of time from process creation to process termination and is measured in clock tics. "Memory usage" is an average usage figure measured in clicks. The size of a click is hardware-dependent.

Characters read or written quantifies the character I/O of the process. Blocks read or written quantifies the block I/O of the process. The command name is the name of the process.

The accounting buffer address and pointer to the inode of the process accounting file facilitate execution of the UNIX kernel accounting program.

Keep in mind that the process accounting file contains mainly binary information and is not intended to be displayed directly. The process accounting records are processed and summarized for you by existing UNIX commands. You simply need to learn how to use the commands provided.

9.3.2 Extracting Useful Information from Process Accounting Data

Acctcms is a command that is used to convert raw process accounting records into useful information. The simplified syntax of the *acctcms* command is:

>   *acctcms* [-s] [-a] file_name... > **outfile**

The "-s" flag indicates that the input file(s) are in summary rather than raw format. The "-a" flag causes the output to be generated in ASCII format so that it can be displayed or printed.

Figure 9.1 shows an example of a shell that would keep a running total of process accounting statistics in file **total** and generate a printable daily process accounting report in file **processreport**. In Figure 9.1 the *acctcms* command is first called to summarize the **pact** file in the **today** file. The old **total** file is renamed **oldtotal**. The *acctcms* command is then called with the "-s" option to combine the summary statistics from the **oldtotal** and **today** files into a new **total** file. Finally, the *acctcms* command is called with the "-a" and "-s" options to generate a printable daily command summary in the **processreport** file.

9.3.3 Advice on Process Accounting

If you need process accounting data, you will probably want to run daily process accounting overnight via a **crontab** entry. The main daily accounting shell procedure is called *runacct* and processes connect, fee, disk, and process accounting files. Generation and analysis of accounting data depend on the needs of the installation. UNIX provides accounting tools that are used by system administrators to gather data and generate reports needed by an installation.

If you turn on the data gathering accounting tools, make sure that you process the data and remove old files. Otherwise you could have a system full of accounting data with no place to put user files!

# Summarize today's data.

acctcms **/usr/adm/pact** **>today**

 # Update summary file for today's data

cp total oldtotal

acctcms -s **today oldtotal>total**

 # Generate printable command summary report for today

acctcms -a -s **today >processreport**

Figure 9.1   Daily Command Accounting Shell

9.4 Monitoring Ports

First, the use of a "port plan" will be described to match port names with physical hardware. Second, monitoring port usage will be discussed.

9.4.1 Using a Port Plan

Whoever installed your system should have left a "port plan" for you to use. A "port plan" is a table showing the name of each port on your system and the transmission media to which it is connected. This document serves as a road map to your understanding of port usage. If a "port plan" is not available, you will need to do a field survey of your hardware and make one up yourself.

A typical port plan for a system with 16 multiplexer ports is shown in Table 9.1. Many multiplexer line boards have eight ports. Numbering in octal, the first digit identifies the line board, and the second digit identifies the port. The first column shows the name of each port. Note that the port

Table 9.1   Port Plan for a Small System

Port Name	Connection	Use
tty00	HW	line printer
tty01	HW	laser printer
tty02	S75	terminal
tty03	S75	terminal
tty04	S75	terminal
tty05	S75	terminal
tty06	S75	terminal
tty07	S75	terminal
tty10	S75	terminal
tty11	S75	terminal
tty12	S75	terminal
tty13	S75	terminal
tty14	S75	terminal
tty15	S75	terminal
tty16	S75	terminal
tty17	S75	terminal

numbers are in octal. The second column shows what the port is connected to. "HW" means that the port is connected to a hard wired line. "S75" indicates that the port is connected to a System 75* PBX. The third column shows what each port is used for. Ports 0 and 1 are for a line printer and laser printer located in the computer room. The System 75 ports provide data service for user terminals located locally or remotely. Note that ports of a given type have been set up so that they will have contiguous entries in the table.

---

*   System 75 is a registered trademark of AT&T.

ADMINISTRATION OF COMPUTING RESOURCES   111

console	console	Dec 3 6:30
fjb	tty02	Dec 3 7:00
drb	tty03	Dec 3 7:53

Figure 9.2   *who* Command Output

9.4.2 Monitoring Port Usage

Port usage may be monitored using the *who* command. The *who* command reports who is on the system. Generally, a system administrator uses the *who* command without arguments to determine who is logged into the system, on which port, and the time logged on.

Figure 9.2 shows output for the *who* command on a lightly loaded system. The three columns show login name, port name, and time of log on. A system administrator must refer to the "port plan" to translate the raw data from Figure 9.2 into useful information on port usage. Figure 9.2 shows the system console, and two System 75 ports in use. Note that the console does not appear in the port plan, since it does not connect to the system through a multiplexer port. Only the ports that have an associated shell running are reported by the *who* command. That is why the ports for the line printer and laser printer do not appear.

A second way in which a system administrator uses the *who* command is with the "-u" option. With this option *who* reports the name of the login, the name of the port being used, the time of log on, the time span since last activity on the port, and the process ID.

Figure 9.3 shows typical output for this command on a loaded system. The first three columns are login name, port name, and time logged on. The fourth column is the time in minutes and seconds since the last terminal activity. If the port has been used in the last minute, a '.' is shown. If the port has not been used in 24 hours or since the last reboot, 'old' is shown. The fifth column shows the process ID of the shell for that port. Using the data from Figure 9.3 and the "port plan,"

console	console	Dec 3 6:30	2:17	2543
jpo	tty17	Dec 3 8:14	0:01	1529
hma	tty16	Dec 3 8:10	0:16	1423
fjb	tty02	Dec 3 7:55	.	1523
jjo	tty03	Dec 3 8:01	.	1345
edm	tty04	Dec 3 6:55	.	1134
jjd	tty10	Dec 3 8:45	1:00	1375
hkp	tty05	Dec 3 8:20	2:13	1724
skb	tty06	Dec 3 8:47	1:45	1379
bas	tty07	Dec 3 9:01	0:07	1381
tpd	tty11	Dec 3 8:03	0:01	1721
jrm	tty12	Dec 3 8:10	.	1720
amh	tty13	Dec 3 8:13	.	1723
rmc	tty15	Dec 3 7:45	.	1421
fas	tty14	Dec 3 7:49	.	1422

Figure 9.3   *who* -u Output

an administrator can see that the 14 System 75 ports in the example system are all in use.

9.5 Identifying Bottlenecks

The *sar* command is invoked to generate system activity reports that define resource problems. The UNIX operating system maintains cumulative activity counters for cpu utilization, buffer activity, block device I/O, terminal device I/O, system calls, swapping, file access, queues, operating system tables, and semaphores.

Sar can be called to sample system activity and display a report on the screen (and optionally store the report in binary format in a file) as follows:

   sar [options] [-o file] t [n]

The "-o" argument is used to specify a file where a binary copy of the report is to be stored. *Sar* will sample system activity at

ADMINISTRATION OF COMPUTING RESOURCES

Table 9.2 *sar* Options

Option	Information Reported
-u	cpu utilization
-b	buffer activity
-d	block device I/O activity
-y	terminal device I/O activity
-c	system calls
-w	swapping and process switches
-a	file accesses
-q	queue length
-v	status of operating system tables
-m	message and semaphore activity
-A	all data

n (default = 1) intervals of t seconds.

Table 9.2 lists the *sar* options used to select the type of data to be reported. Each data selection option in Table 9.2 will cause column headings to be printed. The column headings provide a terse explanation of the data printed. A more detailed explanation is presented on the *sar* (1) manual page. The "-u" and "-d" options on *sar* will be explained since they are commonly used. Most of the other options are seldom used.

9.5.1 Cpu Activity Monitoring

The "-u" option characterizes cpu utilization in terms of the percentage of time running user programs, running system programs, waiting for completion of block I/O, and otherwise idle.

9.5.2 Disk and Tape Drive Activity Monitoring

The "-d" option reports on activity for each block device as follows:

1. The percentage of the time that the device is busy

2. The average number of requests outstanding
3. The total number of reads and writes in the sample period
4. The total number of blocks transferred in the sample period
5. The average waiting time in the queue in milliseconds
6. The average amount of time to complete an I/O activity (seek time plus rotational delay plus transfer time)

Automatic procedures may be set up to gather system activity data as described in the *sar* (1M) manual page. Because most administrators are too busy to examine system activity data in the absence of major problems, it is probably best to gather data only when you need it.

9.6 Solving Computing Resource Problems

Following are suggestions for solving resource problems in the areas of disk space, ports, cpu cycles, and fast memory.

9.6.1 Shortage of Disk Space

When you are low on disk free space, consider the following approaches in the order given:

1. Ask users to remove unneeded files and directories.
2. Implement automated procedures to identify unused files.
3. Reorganize file systems using *dcopy*.
4. Install additional disk drives.

9.6.2 Shortage of Ports

When you are short on multiplexer ports, consider the following approaches:

1. Ask users to log off when they will be away from their terminals for long periods of time.
2. Implement automated procedures to log off inactive terminals.
3. Install additional ports.

9.6.3 Shortage of Cpu Cycles

When you are short on cpu cycles, consider the following approaches:

1. Try to shift work into low usage periods (for example, run incremental file backups in the middle of the night).
2. Install a cpu upgrade.
3. Purchase an additional system.

9.6.4 Shortage of Memory

When you are short on memory, consider the following approaches:

1. Add more memory.
2. Purchase an additional system.

9.7 Summary

Disk usage may be monitored with the *df* command. Cpu usage on a per process basis may be monitored with the *acctcms* command. Port usage can be monitored with the *who* command in conjunction with a "port plan." A "port plan" shows the name of each port, what transmission medium it is connected to, and what it is used for.

Bottlenecks can be identified with the *sar* command. The "-u" option is useful in monitoring cpu activity; the "-d" option is useful in monitoring block device activity.

The standard approaches to solving computing resource problems are:

1. Eliminate unneeded use.
2. Shift use away from peak periods.
3. Purchase more hardware.

9.8 Exercises

1. What disk block sizes are used with various UNIX systems? What disk block size is used with your system?
2. Write a command to determine the number of free blocks and inodes in the /c1 file system.

3. Write a command to determine the number of blocks used for your login directory (and everything in it and beneath it).

4. How do you turn on process accounting in UNIX?

5. What do the "-s" and "-a" arguments of the *acctcms* command do?

6. Write a "port plan" for your system.

7. Find out how many ports are currently being used on your system.

8. Write a command that will tell you the percentage of time that your cpu is idle.

9. Write a command that will tell you the number of blocks transferred to and from each disk drive on your system.

10. What would you do if you found you had a shortage of disk space?

11. What would you do to solve a port shortage problem?

12. Can you think of additional ways to solve a cpu cycle problem beyond those suggested in the chapter? What are they?

13. Are some types of resource shortages more serious than others? Why?

10. PLANNING A SYSTEM CONFIGURATION

OBJECTIVES

After reading this chapter, you should be able to:

1. Describe the major parts of a time-shared computer system.
2. Describe the minimum "reasonable" configuration of a time-shared computer system.
3. Specify requirements for a computer system on a functional basis.
4. Be familiar with the aspects of site preparation for a computer system.

Chapter 10 is intended to help someone who does not yet have a system to design and procure a hardware configuration suited to his or her needs. First, the various components of a hardware configuration will be discussed. Then some "typical" hardware configurations will be examined. Finally, preparing a bid specification and obtaining the needed hardware configuration will be covered.

10.1 Components of a Hardware Configuration

In this section we will list the components making up a hardware configuration and examine some of the considerations in sizing or selecting each individual component. The components to be discussed are:

1. Central processing unit
2. Memory
3. Disk drives

4. Tape drives
5. Multiplexers
6. Networking hardware
7. Printers

I have suggested per user resource allocations based on my experience over the past seven years. The suggestions are geared toward a software development organization operating on a tight schedule. The resource allocation guidelines provide a starting point.

10.1.1 Central Processing Unit

A central processing unit (cpu) is essential to any computer system. The important parameters regarding the choice of a cpu are its speed and the number and nature of I/O channels that it supports.

The speed of a cpu is measured in millions of instructions per second (mips). The power of commercially available cpus ranges from a fraction of a mips to 30 mips. The requirement for computing power grows as the number of users and intensity of use increase. Generally, 1/20 mips per concurrent user should serve as a guideline for most organizations.

A second important characteristic of a cpu is the number of I/O channels, or buses, that it has associated with it. Sufficient capacity must be available to handle all the disk, tape, memory, and network controllers that will be required. The word size of modern cpus and the size of the buses linking the cpu and memory is 32 bits wide.

10.1.2 Memory

Random access memory (ram) is another essential component of any computer system. Size is the key memory parameter. It is important to know the maximum amount of memory that can be installed on a computer system. Not only do you want the computer system to be able to handle your immediate needs, but you also want the system to be able to grow as your needs expand.

Memory is measured in megabytes. The memory size of commercially available computers ranges from a fraction of a

PLANNING A SYSTEM CONFIGURATION   119

megabyte to around 64 megabytes. The requirement for memory grows as the number of users and the intensity of use increase. 1/10 megabyte of ram per concurrent user should be sufficient for most uses.

10.1.3 Disk Drives

At least one disk drive is essential to any computer system. Because disk drives have moving parts that are subject to relatively frequent failure, a hardware configuration should have at least two disk drives. In a multiple disk drive configuration, the failure of a disk drive does not mean a failure of the whole computer system.

Several important factors should be considered in choosing disk drives:

1. Storage capacity of the drive in megabytes
2. Transfer rate in kilobytes per second
3. Whether the disk media is fixed or removable

You will need to consider the amount of disk storage capacity that you need to determine how many disk drives to include in your hardware configuration. A suggested rule of thumb is to have a drive for your operating system, a spare drive that can host the operating system in an emergency, and enough additional drives to provide 20 megabytes of storage capacity per active user. The storage capacity of disk drives ranges from 100 to 1,000 megabytes.

A hardware configuration should have at least one disk drive with removable media. A removable media drive greatly facilitates the implementation of an effective file backup strategy and eases the transfer of large amounts of information between systems.

10.1.4 Tape Drives

At least one tape drive is essential to any hardware configuration; the UNIX operating system and most utilities are distributed on tape. Tape drives play a role in the file backup strategy for many hardware configurations.

The important characteristics of a tape drive are ease of use, recording density, and transfer rate. Generally, a self loading tape drive with as fast a transfer rate as possible should be chosen. Most small and medium sized computer systems have only one tape drive. Large systems, and systems with all fixed media disk drives may have two or more tape drives to facilitate file backup.

10.1.5 Multiplexers

The multiplexer supports ports using the RS232C interface. The key parameters of the multiplexer are the number of ports that it supports and the baud rates to which the ports can be set. Typically, support for 300, 1200, 2400, 4800, and 9600 baud is needed. Enough ports must be installed to handle the projected number of concurrent users for your system. It is a good idea to allow a 20 percent margin of extra ports to be sure your users have enough working ports.

10.1.6 Networking Hardware

Any computer should have the capability to communicate with distant computers. This type of communication is carried out by a "wide area network."

In a multiple computer installation, the various computers in the installation should be able to communicate with each other. This type of communication is carried out by a "local area network."

Wide Area Network
In order to give your computer the capability to dial up another computer, you will need one or more automatic dialing units that can be controlled by the computer. Each of these dialing units is connected to a central office phone line. With this configuration you will be able to conduct low speed (1200 baud) file transfers between your computer and any other computer with dial-up phone ports (assuming you have a login and password for the other computer). With the equipment noted above you will be able to use the UNIX commands *cu* and *uucp*.

The important parameter regarding the wide area network is the number of concurrent login sessions on distant computers that you expect.

Local Area Network
A multiple computer facility usually ties its computers together in a local area network to facilitate intercomputer communication. Each computer has an adapter or interface unit that is joined to the others by a twisted pair of wires, coaxial cable, or fiber optics cable. These networks provide high speed (1–20 million bits per second) file transfers.

For example, the *nusend* file transfer command can be run using equipment obtained from the Network Systems Company (NSC). The *nisend* file transfer command can be run using equipment obtained from the Interlan Company.

The important parameters in the choice of a local area network are the number of bytes of information that must be transferred between computers, how quickly a transfer must be completed, the allowable transmission error rate, and the required reliability and availability of the network.

10.1.7 Printers

The two large classes of printers are mechanical line printers and laser printers. Most installations need at least one printer of each type.

The important parameters regarding printing are print quality and print speed. The cost per page of line printer output is relatively low, but the print quality is also usually mediocre. The cost per page of laser printer output is higher, but print quality is very good.

10.2 Typical Configurations

Three different computing environments will be examined as examples of typical configurations: (a) a college computer science department; (b) a software house; and (c) a professional group. These situations were chosen because they differ in number of users and the nature of use. A hardware configuration will be proposed for each situation based on the guidelines suggested in the chapter.

10.2.1 A Typical Configuration for a Computer Science Department

Assume that a college computer science department has 400 undergraduate students and that no more than 60 are logged in

Table 10.1   System Configuration for a Computer Science Department

COMPONENT	NUMBER	DESCRIPTION	COMMENT
CPU	3	Mips	
Memory	6	Mbytes	
Disk	2	Drives	Fixed Media
Tape	1	Drive	
Multiplexer	96	Ports	
Wide Area Network	2	Lines	
Laser Printers	1	Printer	
Line Printers	1	Printer	

at any one time. The department further breaks down into 200 computer science majors, who use the computer for several courses, and 200 students of other majors, who are taking a computer literacy course. The suggested configuration is shown in Table 10.1.

The undergraduate academic environment is characterized by large numbers of light to moderate users. The suggested configuration has a cpu with 3 mips and 6 megabytes of memory based on the suggested cpu cycle and memory allocation per concurrent user. There is no local area network because this is a single computer installation. The other components are listed at the minimum level.

10.2.2 Software House

Assume a software house has 100 employees, most of whom hold graduate degrees in computer science. All 100 users have intensive use and are logged on continuously during prime shift. The software house has been in business for several years, and users edit existing source files and initiate compiles that may take an hour or more to complete. Two computers are suggested, each configured as shown in Table 10.2.

PLANNING A SYSTEM CONFIGURATION

Table 10.2   System Configuration for a Software House

COMPONENT	NUMBER	DESCRIPTION	COMMENT
CPU	2.5	Mips	
Memory	5	Mbytes	
Disk	4	Drives	3 Fixed, 1 Removable
Tape	1	Drive	
Multiplexer	64	Ports	
Local Area Network	1	Network	
Wide Area Network	4	Lines	
Laser Printers	1	Printer	
Line Printers	1	Printer	

The software house computing environment is characterized by a moderate number of intensive computer users. There would be a large economic impact if computing resources were unavailable, or if files were lost.

This organization has two computers. If one goes down, work will continue in a degraded fashion on the other system. A removable media disk drive is provided on each system to allow for daily file backup activities.

Each computer in this configuration has 2.5 mips and 5 megabytes, which is half the need of the organization. Four lines are provided on each system to allow programmers to dial up their customers' systems or dial in from home. The two computers are joined together with a local area network to allow high speed file transfer between them.

10.2.3 Small Business

Assume that a professional office has four employees who use the computer and that they are all logged on concurrently. Assume that the users execute "canned" programs such as database systems, and text processors.

Table 10.3   System Configuration for a Professional Office

COMPONENT	NUMBER	DESCRIPTION	COMMENT
CPU	.2	Mips	
Memory	1	Mbyte	
Disk	2	Drives	1 hard, 1 floppy
Multiplexer	4	Ports	
Wide Area Network	1	Line	
Line Printer	1	Printer	

A single computer is suggested, configured as shown in Table 10.3.

This configuration falls into the range covered by a "personal computer." Although the computer is used continuously on prime shift, usage is light. One of the users would use the keyboard of the personal computer, and the other three would use terminals.

In this case, we cannot strictly apply the suggested formulas. One megabyte of fast memory is needed in order to run many software packages that a small business might want to use. We have suggested one megabyte of fast memory because of software imposed requirements.

10.3 Preparing a Bid Specification

In order to prepare a bid specification you need to gather information, develop a system configuration specification, and select appropriate benchmarks.

10.3.1 Sources of Information

Technical experts within your own company, users you know within other companies, consultants, and computer salespeople are all good sources of information on configuration planning.

In-House
You should obtain information on projected use from the prospective users of your computer. If you work for a large company, you may be able to call on technical experts for help or possibly some other organization that already has a configuration similar to the one you are planning. When considering a system, it is particularly valuable to be able to talk to someone who already has one in use.

Other Users
Through your membership in professional and trade organizations you may know people who already have a system like the one you are planning. Usually, salespeople can give you the name of a user with a configuration similar to the one you are planning. It is worthwhile to locate users of a similar configuration and find out if they are satisfied with it and what problems they have experienced.

Consultants
If you are unable to get the information you need through your own organization or through your peers in other companies, you might consider using a consultant who has experience dealing with applications like your own.

Salespeople
Salespeople are happy to provide you with information about their products. Generally, salespeople are backed up by marketing support people who are technical experts on their product line. They will be willing to propose a configuration that they feel will meet your needs.

Although a salesperson's goal is to sell you his or her system, salespeople also want to create a happy customer who will facilitate further sales rather than discourage them. You can double check their claims with other users inside and outside your company or with a consultant. *In no case* should a salesperson be your only source of information. You should always talk to prior customers, consultants, or other vendors to get multiple viewpoints on a salesperson's proposed solution to your problem.

10.3.2 System Configuration Specification

The worksheet in Table 10.4 can be used to specify your basic computer configuration. You will need to fill in the number

Table 10.4   System Configuration Worksheet

COMPONENT	NUMBER	DESCRIPTION	COMMENT
CPU		Mips	
Memory		Mbytes	
Disk		Drives	
Tape		Drives	
Multiplexer		Ports	
Laser Printers		Printers	
Line Printers		Printers	

column with the number of each component required. You will also need to specify detailed device-specific information in the comment section (for example, the number of blocks that a disk drive is to be capable of storing). The specific parameters that need to be specified for each component are discussed earlier in the chapter.

10.3.3 Benchmarks

Several benchmarks should be selected, and performance against these benchmarks should be specified. The benchmarks should be selected to be similar to the type of work that will be done on your configuration. For a start, the following benchmarks are suggested:

1. Compiling of a 200 line 'C' program
2. Formatting a 100 line *nroff* source file
3. Executing a shell with 10 of the most commonly used UNIX commands

The maximum allowable execution time for each of the above benchmarks should be specified in milliseconds.

10.4 Obtaining Your System

To obtain your proposed system, you will need to locate a number of qualified computer vendors and, through your purchasing and legal departments, request bids and negotiate a purchase contract.

10.4.1 Evaluating Vendors

You should examine the following characteristics when you compare vendors:

1. Proximity of a sales/technical support office
2. Hardware and software availability from the same vendor
3. Availability of hardware and software support
4. Proximity of a service office
5. Stable operating history of the company
6. Maturity of the company's product line
7. Prior experience with the vendor

10.4.2 Bid and Contract Procedure

Obtaining bids from at least three qualified vendors increases your chance of getting a good price on your system. Your company's purchasing and legal departments should be involved in setting up the bid procedure and writing the contract with the successful bidder.

10.5 Site Preparation

Site preparation entails providing for the physical needs of a computer system. The space to house the system must be obtained. Electrical power of the proper voltage and amperage must be installed. Provision needs to be made to keep the computer's environment within the manufacturer's specifications for temperature and humidity. Many computer manufacturers provide a site preparation guide to assist with planning the site.

10.6 Summary

A computer system consists of a central processing unit, fast memory, multiplexers, disk drives, tape drives, printers, and networking hardware.

Every computer system has a central processing unit. The power of the cpu is measured in the number of millions of instructions per second (mips) that it can execute. Likewise, every computer has fast memory. The amount of fast memory is measured in megabytes.

One or more disk drives are attached to a computer system to provide long-term storage in the hundreds of megabytes range. Information stored on disk can be accessed in tens of milliseconds and remains even during a power outage.

A tape drive is attached to a minicomputer-sized computer system to provide long-term storage of large quantities of information. Minicomputer software is typically distributed on tape.

Multiplexers allow users to communicate with a computer system from their terminals via hard wired lines or the telephone system. Some multiplexers support only one communications speed and others support a range of speeds from 300 baud to 19.2 K baud.

Printers allow users to obtain a paper copy of their results. The two major kinds of printers are line printers and laser printers. Line printers provide high volume, cheap, low quality output. Laser printers provide low volume, high quality output.

Networking hardware may be as simple as an autodialer, dataset, and telephone line or may involve complex hardware and software. Networking hardware allows communication among computer systems.

A UNIX PC might be configured with a 20 megabyte hard disk, a megabyte of fast memory, and an autodialer. The central processing unit would operate at a few tenths mips.

A 3B20 might be configured with several high capacity disk drives, a tape drive, 8 megabytes of fast memory, and a high speed local area network bus. The central processing unit would operate at approximately one mip.

You may analytically determine the size of the system that you need. I use factors of 1/20 mips per user, 1/10 megabyte of fast memory per user, and 20 megabytes of disk storage per user. Obviously, a user needs a port to log on to. Printing and networking requirements are highly user dependent. In this chapter we provided configuration examples of a college computer science department, a software house, and a professional office.

Obtaining a computer system is a formal procedure that involves a company's purchasing and legal departments as well as its computer center. The computer center is expected to write objective requirements or specifications for a new computer system. Technical experts within your company, colleagues at local companies, consultants, and computer sales representatives can help provide information for the system specification.

Before a computer can be installed, provision must be made to provide space, power, and a suitable environment.

10.7 Exercises

1. Determine the computing power available to each concurrent user of your college's UNIX system. How do the per user cpu allocation and memory allocation compare to the figures suggested in this chapter?

2. Why should a computer system have at least two disk drives?

3. Why should a computer system have a tape drive?

4. Why should a computer system have more multiplexer ports than users?

5. Determine if your system is capable of dialing into other UNIX systems. How many concurrent login sessions on distant computers are possible? What hardware is used to implement this capability?

6. Find out if your system has a local area network. What is the name and model of the local area network hardware? Is the network based on coaxial cable, twisted pairs of wire, or fiber optics cable?

7. Is it always safe to use the resource requirement factors suggested in this chapter? Why or why not?

8. Specify a system configuration for a 100-student high school mathematics department. No more than 20 students will use the computer concurrently.

9. Specify benchmarks that you could use for the system in Exercise 8.

10. Discuss some of the advantages and disadvantages of using one large computer rather than several small computers.

11. Propose benchmarks for use with the three case studies in the chapter: (a) the computer science department, (b) the software house, and (c) the small business.

12. What are the important considerations in preparing a site for a new computer?

11. SYSTEM GENERATION OVERVIEW

OBJECTIVES

After reading this chapter, you should be able to:

1. Explain a UNIX system generation.
2. Explain why system generation is hardware specific.
3. Name the document that contains complete system generation instructions for the 3B20S.
4. Describe the functions of the Emergency Action Interface.
5. Describe how UNIX is distributed.
6. List the major steps in a system generation.

In this chapter we offer an overview of the steps involved in doing a UNIX SYSTEM V system generation for an AT&T 3B20S* minicomputer. System generation is the process of making an operating system for a specific hardware configuration, and is a complex task that is usually performed by an experienced system administrator.

11.1 Hardware Configuration

A universal system generation procedure does not exist. The details of the procedure differ depending on the hardware vendor, the specific model computer, and the hardware options chosen.

---

* 3B20S is a registered trademark of AT&T.

Table 11.1 3B20S Minimum Hardware Configuration

Hardware Device	Quantity
Memory	1 MB
Direct Memory Access Channels	1
Disk File Controller	1
Moving Head Disks	2
I/O Processor	1
Tape Controller (UN32)	1
Tape Drive	1
Console (TN83)	1
TTY420	1
8 Line Async. Multiplexer (TN4)	1

We shall use the AT&T 3B20S to illustrate this chapter. This is a superminicomputer-sized system, whose system generation involves all the significant aspects of system generation. A minimum configuration 3B20S, as defined in Table 11.1, will be used for illustration. This configuration allows for eight users and has been chosen for educational purposes only. Typical configurations with the 3B20S cpu average 30 users.

The system generation of a VAX 780* has analogous steps. The procedure described here is a model for system generation of UNIX SYSTEM V on a minicomputer-sized system.

11.2 Documentation

We shall limit ourselves in this chapter to providing an overview of system generation for the 3B20S. After reading this chapter, if you are charged with doing a system generation, you should obtain a copy of the following document: *UNIX*

---

* VAX is a registered trademark of Digital Equipment Corporation.

SYSTEM GENERATION OVERVIEW 133

SYSTEM V Release 2.0 Administrative Guide for 3B20S Computers (AT&T, 1983). An *Administrative Guide* has been available for each minicomputer that runs UNIX SYSTEM V. The *Administrative Guide* for a system is indispensable to planning and implementing a system generation.

11.3 Prerequisites

The system administrator must be familiar with the operation of the system console, Emergency Action Interface (EAI), tape drive, and disk drive, since these are necessary to generate a system. Such knowledge is generally acquired through on-the-job training.

The minimum hardware configuration should be fully operational. A vendor customer engineer running stand-alone diagnostic programs can verify that this is the case.

The system administrator must have a complete detailed description of the entire hardware configuration, including controller channel and device addresses, peripheral controller slots, disk locations, and memory type. The vendor technician who installed the system or the site guide for the system can supply this information. A site guide is a log book, kept for a computer system, that specifies the hardware that was initially installed and any changes that were made to the hardware.

11.4 The Emergency Action Interface

The Emergency Action Interface (EAI) of the 3B20S is built into the system console, a specially equipped Dataspeed 40* terminal. The system console interfaces to the 3B20S processor through the Maintenance TTY Peripheral Controller (MTTYPC). The EAI is used for initial loading, booting, reconfiguring, and halting the 3B20S.

The system console has a CRT screen and a keyboard. The keyboard has the standard set of keys for 128 character ASCII input, plus a set of four EAI special function keys. When the system console is in EAI mode, the CRT has several

---

* Dataspeed 40 is a registered trademark of AT&T.

Table 11.2   EAI Keys on System Console

EA DISP	Starts Emergency Action Mode
NORM DISP	Ends Emergency Action Mode
CMD/MSG	Toggles Cursor Between EAI and UNIX Areas of Screen
ALM RLS	Currently Unused

EAI areas and a normal UNIX terminal area.

11.4.1 EAI Special Function Keys

The EAI keys are shown in Table 11.2. The EAI DISP key starts emergency action mode. The NORM DISP key terminates emergency action mode. The CMD/MSG key toggles the cursor between the EAI command area and the UNIX terminal area of the screen. The ALM RLS key is currently unused.

11.4.2 EAI Screen Areas

Table 11.3 shows the layout of the system console when it is in EAI mode. EAI status, menu display areas, and a command input area are shown, along with a normal UNIX terminal area.

Brief EAI command names and corresponding command numbers are displayed in the **EAI menu display area**.

System status is shown in the **EAI status indicator area**. Of particular interest in the status area are the EAI flag, which indicates whether the EAI can communicate with the MTTYPC, and the PRM indicator, which provides the Processor Recovery Message that indicates EAI command success or failure.

EAI commands can only be entered when the cursor is positioned in the **EAI command input area**. The cursor is toggled between the EAI command area and the UNIX

Table 11.3   System Console Layout in EAI Mode

EAI Command Input Area
EAI Status Indicator Area
EAI Menu Display Area
Normal UNIX Terminal Area

terminal area with the CMD/MSG function key.

Once UNIX is running, the **UNIX terminal area** provides a normal UNIX terminal display. The CMD/MSG function key toggles the cursor between this area and the EAI command area. When UNIX is up, this area and the keyboard serve as a normal UNIX terminal.

11.5 Initial Loading and Booting

UNIX SYSTEM V is distributed on magnetic tape, recorded in 9-track format, usually at 1600 bits per inch density. A UNIX distribution contains from three to four reels of tape, called distribution tapes. It is important that you check that your tapes are externally marked 3B20S; trying to install UNIX with the wrong set of tapes would be time consuming and without result.

11.5.1 Organization of the Distribution Tapes

Tape 0 contains the initial load program and selectable items.

Tape 1 contains a copy of the root file system in physical format. Root is also known as /, which is the root of the UNIX hierarchical file structure. The root file system contains the commands needed to generate the system. We should have selected the tape 1 reel for our specific type of disk drive from the two versions of the tape 1 reel in the distribution.

Tape 2 contains the /usr file system in *cpio* format (2048 byte records). The /usr file system must be mounted on a system when it is in multiuser mode since it contains programs used by ordinary users.

Tape 3 is contained only in an update release, which means that only selected files are changing. Here we assume that we are dealing with a complete release and that no tape 3 is in the distribution.

11.5.2 Loading Tape 1

The Emergency Action Interface (EAI) is used to load the initial load program and the root file system, which reside on tape 1. The EAI menu screen is brought up on the system console by pressing the EAI DISP button on the console keyboard. Tape 1 is mounted on the tape drive and the EAI LDTAPE command is executed to copy the initial load program and the root file system from the tape drive to the selected moving head disk. Moving head disk 0 is the target if the SEC-DISK flag is clear, and moving head disk 1 is the target if the flag is set. If the PARAMETER field on the EAI screen contains an f or F, the target disk will be formatted before the tape is loaded. If the PARAMETER field is blank, the operator will be asked if the disk is to be formatted.

The PARAMETER field values used herein assume the tape drive is device 2 on channel 11. If the tape drive is located at a different location, see the ldtape(8) manual page for appropriate values.

The tape will be copied to disk, the tape rewound, and assuming success, a Processor Recovery Message (PRM) will be issued indicating that the load was successful. Should an error occur, a PRM will be issued indicating the problem. The PRM(8) manual page explains PRM error codes.

11.5.3 Booting UNIX

Several versions of UNIX, corresponding to the various supported tape controllers, are contained in the root file system. Our example configuration has a un32 high-speed CIPHER tape controller. We thus need to boot /unix.un32.

The EAI is used to boot UNIX. The MIN-CONFIG and PROMPT-UNIX options must be set on the EAI to allow choice of the appropriate UNIX. The MIN-CONFIG flag causes UNIX to bring up only the system console, the boot device, a tape drive, and the first megabyte of main memory. The BOOT command is issued on the EAI screen, and the response to the UNIX selection prompt is /unix.un32, in this case.

11.5.4 Taking Precautions

The root file system is checked with /etc/fsck to ensure its integrity. The appropriate system file (in this case /etc/system.un32) is copied to /etc/system. A copy of the root file system is placed in the backup root file system area (section 7) of disk 0 so that you are able to easily boot the system if the primary root file system becomes corrupted.

11.6 Initial Load of /usr File System

The /usr file system is on tape 2 in *cpio* format (2048 byte records). The /usr file system must be mounted for the system to go to multi-user mode.

Tape 2 is mounted on tape drive 0 and positioned at its load point. An empty file system is mounted as /usr. You can mount /usr wherever you like, provided you modify /etc/checklist appropriately. The shell script in Figure 11.1 mounts /usr on section 1 of disk 0.

11.7 Initial Load of Selectable Items

Tape 0 contains a load tape-to-disk program and four *cpio* files in the following order:

1. Load tape to disk program
2. On line manual pages
3. On line documents
4. Remote Job Entry (RJE) software.

The load tape to disk program is several 512 byte records. The *cpio* files have 2048 byte records. The shell program shown in Figure 11.2 skips the tape-to-disk program, installs the on line

mkfs **/dev/rdsk/0s1** 900000 7 608

labelit **/dev/rdsk/0s1** usr pack23

fsck **/dev/rdsk/0s1**

mount **/dev/rdsk/0s1 /usr**

chmod 775 **/usr**

cd **/usr**

dd if=**/dev/rmt/0m** bs=2048 | *cpio* -idm

Figure 11.1 Shell Script to Mount and Load the /usr File System

manual pages, and documents and rewinds the tape. The RJE software is not loaded, as it is not needed for our system.

11.8 Special Files

Special files provide a consistent, easy to use method of input and output. End users take their input from or direct their output to a special file. The system administrators must make sure that a special file exists for each peripheral device in their configuration; many are already provided on the root distribution tape, but some must be made by the system administrators.

11.8.1 Types of Special Files

Two kinds of special files exist—character special files and block special files. Character special files are used for serial character at a time I/O. A multiplexer port for a user terminal is an example of a character special file. Block special files are used for block at a time I/O. A tape drive is an example of a block special file. For each block special file there is also a "raw" special file that allows the block device to be accessed as

SYSTEM GENERATION OVERVIEW

skip load program

echo **</dev/rmt0mn**

install manual pages

cd **/usr**

mkdir **catman**

chown bin **catman**

chmod 755 **catman**

dd if=**/dev/rmt0mn** bs=2048 | *cpio* -idm

#install documents

cd **/usr**

mkdir **docs**

chown bin **docs**

chmod 755 **docs**

dd if=**/dev/rmt/0m** bs=2048 | *cpio* idm

Figure 11.2 Shell Script to Load Selectable Files

a character special device.

11.8.2 Device Numbers

I/O devices in UNIX are accessed by two integer numbers, called major and minor device numbers. Each special file is associated with a major and minor device number. The major device number normally corresponds to device driver for a physical piece of hardware like a disk drive. The minor device number can correspond to a subset of a physical piece of hardware, like a section of a disk drive, or may correspond to a particular mode of operation of a piece of hardware like a tape drive rewinding after an I/O operation.

11.8.3 Examining Special Files

The special files are contained in the /**dev** directory. You can change directory to /**dev** and do an *ls* -l command and you will see a listing that looks like Figure 11.3. The first character on each line of the listing in Figure 11.3 is the type of device: 'c' for character and 'b' for block. The two integers separated by a ',' are the major and minor device numbers. The rest of the fields have the standard meanings: permissions, link count, owner, modification date, and file name.

11.8.4 Making Special Files

Special files are created using the /*etc*/*mknod* command. The syntax of the command is:

/*etc*/*mknod*   file_name file_type major minor

where "file_name" is the name of the special file, "file_type" is 'b' for block or 'c' for character, and "major" and "minor" are the major and minor device numbers. The /**etc**/**master** file provides the information needed to determine major and minor device numbers.

All the special files needed for our sample 3B20S configuration are provided on the root distribution tape. The action taken to make the console entry is:

/*etc*/*mknod*   console   c 0 0

Chapter 3 of the *Administrator's Guide for 3B20S Computers* describes commonly available hardware devices for the 3B20S and how to compute major and minor device

```
crw- -w- -w- 1 root sys 0,0 Jan 9 console
crw-r- -r- - 1 root sys 2,0 Jan 9 mem
crw-r- -r- - 1 root sys 2,1 Jan 9 kmem
```

Figure 11.3   Partial ls -l Listing

numbers for each specific device.

11.9 System Description File

The system description file contains information about the hardware configuration, system dependent parameters, and software drivers for a specific system. The system file on the distribution tape is /etc/system.

The format of the system file is that hardware configuration information comes first, followed by a line with only a '$' in column 1, followed by system dependent information. System dependent information includes system devices, system parameters, and software drivers.

11.9.1 Hardware Configuration

Hardware configuration information specific to the 3B20S minicomputer is described in the system(4) manual page.

11.9.2 System Parameters

System parameters alter the size of UNIX tables and control structures and are set based on anticipated system load. The **system** file on the distribution tape contains default values for a system with a medium load. Table 11.4 lists and briefly describes selected system parameters. The sizes of many UNIX internal tables are set at the time UNIX is made. Should the parameters be adjusted, a new UNIX would have to be made for them to take effect. The analogy between a source file and the corresponding object file is appropriate. The parameters correspond to the dimension of arrays of structures.

11.9.3 Software Drivers

The software driver area of the **system** file lists the names of the drivers and the number of instances of multiple instance

Table 11.4 Selected System Parameters

Parameter Name	Description
Buffers	File System I/O Buffers
Inodes	In Memory Inodes
Files	Open File Table Entries
Mounts	Size of Mount Table
Procs	Process Table Entries
Clists	Character List Buffers
Maxproc	Max. Processes Per Regular User

drivers.

11.10 Making UNIX

At this point we are nearly ready to make UNIX. We change directory to **/usr/src/uts/3b/cf**, edit the file **Makefile**, and provide our system name next to the SYS symbol and our node name next to the NODE symbol. The system name is used by *uname*, and the node name is used by *uucp*. Both our system and node name might be mt3bc, for example.

Assuming that we have edited the **/etc/system** file to make any needed changes to the default hardware configuration and system parameters, we would now execute the */etc/config* command, which would read the **/etc/system** and **/etc/master** files and output a **config.c** file that has all the necessary configuration specific information.

We can now make UNIX by typing:

   make VER=version

where "version" is the version number, such as 0125, which could be used to identify a UNIX instance made on January 25. The name of the UNIX that we made would be the concatenation of the system name and the version. In our

SYSTEM GENERATION OVERVIEW 143

example, we would have a UNIX named mt3bc0125.

We test our system by issuing the following commands:

cp   /usr/src/uts/3b/mt3bc0125   /

cd /

unmount   /dev/dsk/0s1

mv /unix /unix.old

ln mt3bc0125   /unix

sync

We halt the system and reboot it. Our UNIX could be started either by the name /unix or by the name mt3bc0125. An old system could be started by referring to its actual name.

11.11 Summary

System generation is the process of making UNIX for a specific hardware configuration and expected load pattern. In order to do a system generation, a detailed description of the hardware configuration must be obtained from the site guide for the system or from the hardware vendor technician. The **/etc/system** file must be edited to show the hardware configuration and expected load.

Anyone planning to do a system generation for a 3B20S computer should obtain the document *UNIX System V Release 2.0 Administrator Guide for 3B20S Computers* and refer to Chapter 3 for detailed instructions.

The Emergency Action Interface (EAI) includes a system console with an enhanced keyboard and display and an interface to the 3B20S processor. The EAI allows loading, booting, halting, reconfiguring, and debugging the system.

UNIX is distributed as a set of magnetic tapes called distribution tapes. In a complete release, one tape contains the root file system, another contains the /usr file system, and a third contains selectable items.

The steps involved in a UNIX system generation are:

1. Initial loading of the root tape
2. Booting a primitive UNIX
3. Loading the /usr tape
4. Loading selectable items such as manual pages and on line documents
5. Making special files
6. Adjusting the system description file
7. Making a configuration file
8. Making UNIX for this configuration.

11.12 Exercises

1. What is a UNIX system generation?
2. Why is a system generation hardware dependent?
3. What document contains complete system generation information for a 3B20S?
4. What are the special keys and screen areas of the Emergency Action Interface on the 3B20S?
5. What are the functions of the Emergency Action Interface?
6. How is UNIX distributed?
7. What are the major steps in a system generation?
8. What are the three major parts of the **system** file?
9. What is a special file? What are the different types of special files?
10. What system parameter controls the maximum number of files that can be open concurrently?
11. What steps must you take to make a change in a system parameter take effect?

12. NETWORK ADMINISTRATION

OBJECTIVES

After reading this chapter, you should be able to:

1. Explain how to use the *uucp* networking capability of UNIX.
2. Draw a block diagram of the hardware used by the *uucp* network.
3. Name the programs that support *uucp* and the major job of each.
4. Name the major files used by *uucp* and the data contained in each.
5. Have a general understanding of how to install *uucp*.
6. Understand the precautions that need to be taken to run *uucp* in a secure manner.
7. Know where to get more detailed information on *uucp* installation and maintenance.

12.1 Network Introduction

Uucp is a system of programs, files, and hardware that provides low cost, low speed networking capability among UNIX systems. Two major features of *uucp* are file transfer between systems and the remote execution of a command on another system. Users access network features through user interface programs that queue work requests.

Uucp supports both dial-up and hard wired connections. Dial-up connections are at 300, 1200, or 2400 baud (roughly 30, 120 or 240 characters per second). Hard wired connections can be at 300, 1200, 9,600, or 19,200 baud.

12.2 User Interface Commands

The *uucp* command provides a user interface for file transfers, the *uux* command provides a user interface for remote execution, the *uuname* command provides a list of known remote systems, and the *uustat* and *uulog* commands provide status information. This chapter is based on the HONEYDANBER version of *Uucp*.

12.2.1 *Uucp*

The *uucp* command allows for files to be copied from one UNIX system to another. The command queues the request for later execution. The syntax of the command is:

uucp [options] <source files> <destination file>

A file name may be a path name on the local machine or may be of the form

system-name!path-name

where "system-name" may be any system that *uucp* knows about. "Path-name" may be a full path name or one of several other options specified on the *uucp* manual page. *Uucp* can be used effectively without options. For example,

uucp myfile b!/a1/gp1/jjs

will send the file **myfile** on the local system to directory **/a1/gp1/jjs** on system 'b'.

12.2.2 *Uux*

The *uux* command allows a command to be executed on a remote UNIX system. The syntax of the *uux* command is:

> *uux* [options] <command-string>

For security reasons, it is customary to strictly limit the set of commands that can be executed by *uux*. The *uux* command can be used effectively without options. Available options are explained on the *uux* manual page. The "<command string>" can contain *uucp* style file names and full path names of commands prefixed with the system name on which they are to be executed. If <command string> contains shell metacharacters, it should be surrounded by double quotes. For example:

> $ uux "a!/bin/who >!a.who"

will execute a *who* command on system 'a' and store the output in file **a.who** on the local system.

12.2.3 *Uuname*

Uuname provides a list of known systems. The syntax of the *uuname* command is:

> uuname

12.2.4 *Uustat*

Uustat provides for *uucp* status inquiries and job control. The syntax of *uustat* is:

> *uustat* [options]

When no options are specified, *uustat* provides status of all the user's *uucp* jobs. The "-q" option lists status information on the job queues for each destination system.

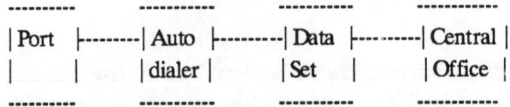

Figure 12.1   Active Site Hardware

12.2.5 *Uulog*

The *uulog* command prints the contents of system log files. It can be called with arguments "-s<system>" and "-u<user>" to limit the report to information about a specific remote system or jobs associated with a specific login. When no arguments are specified, information is printed about all jobs.

12.3 Hardware Overview

Very little hardware must be purchased in order to support *uucp*. Every minicomputer or larger-sized UNIX system already has multiplexer ports. Most UNIX systems already have data sets installed on a number of multiplexer ports.

Uucp sites are classified as active (able to call other sites) or passive (able to be called by other sites).

12.3.1 Active Site Hardware

An active site must have an autodialer in addition to at least one data set connected to a central office (standard) phone line. The autodialer must interface properly to your computer equipment. The make and model required depends on the make of computer you are using. Figure 12.1 shows the hardware required for an active site. Several manufacturers make data sets and autodialers compatible with *uucp*. We will use the AT&T 212 data set and 801 autodialer for illustration in this chapter. The AT&T 2224 data set contains the functionality of both the data set and autodialer modules of the block diagram.

NETWORK ADMINISTRATION

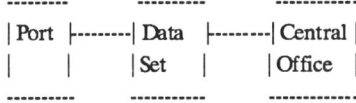

Figure 12.2   Passive Site Hardware

12.3.2 Passive Site Hardware

A passive site needs only a data set connected to a central office phone line. Figure 12.2 shows the hardware required for a passive site.

12.4 Program Overview

Several programs execute in the background to implement networking capability. Table 12.1 lists the major programs involved and their function.

12.4.1 *Uucico*

The *uucico* program performs the following functions:

1. Scans the local spool directory for work
2. Places a call to each remote system for which there is work
3. Negotiates a communications protocol with each remote system
4. Executes and logs transmission requests for the local and remote systems

Uucico is started every time someone initiates a *uucp* command and can be started by a **cron** entry.

Remote systems log into the local system as "nuucp." The system administrator specifies *uucico* in the shell field of the "nuucp" login in order to give remote systems the ability to start *uucico*. The local system administrator needs to inform

Table 12.1   *Uucp* Programs

Program	Description
uucico	handles data transmission between systems
uuxqt	handles remote execution
uuclean	cleans up *uucp* work files

the remote sites of the "nuucp" password so that they may log into the local system.

12.4.2 *Uuxqt*

The *uuxqt* program executes files created by *uux*. *Uuxqt* can be started by either *uux* or *uucico*. The *uuxqt* program scans the spool directory for execute files, performs sanity checking, and, if all right, executes each request.

12.4.3 *Uuclean*

Uuclean removes "old" files from the spool directory. *Uuclean* is generally started by a system daemon once each day.

12.5 File Overview

A number of files and directories are essential to *uucp* operation. Table 12.2 lists the major files and directories and the purpose of each.

12.5.1 Spool Directory

The "spool" directory is **/usr/spool/uucppublic.** This directory is used to hold the work files for *uucp* data transfer and remote execution.

12.5.2 Systems File

The **Systems** file is contained in the **/usr/lib/uucp** directory. The former name for this file was **L.sys.** Each line specifies a remote system that the local system is able to call. An entry in the **Systems** file has the following syntax:

Table 12.2   *Uucp* Files and Directories

File	Description
/usr/spool/uucppublic	"spool" directory to hold work files
/usr/src/cmd/uucp	directory holding source files for *uucp*
/usr/lib/uucp	directory holding system programs and files
Systems	system names and calling instructions
Devices	list of available lines and ACUs
Dialcodes	list of location abbreviations and phone numbers

System   Time   Device   Speed   Phone   Login   Password

"Time" is the allowable time to call and specifies day of the week (Mo, Tu, We, Th, Fr, Sa, Su; "wk" for any weekday and "any" for any day) and time of day (000 = midnight and 1200 = noon).

"Device" is the type of autodialer. ACU is used for the AT&T 801 device. The *uucp* chapter of the *Administrator's Guide* for your system specifies the manufacturer and model number of other supported autodialers.

"Speed" is the line speed (300, 1200, 9600, 19200, or Any).

"Phone" is the phone number of the system and may contain digits (for example, 957−1234) and abbreviations (for example nyc).

Login information is provided as a series of expect-send pairs. "Expect" is what is expected from the remote system, and "send" is what the local system will send in response.

A typical entry in the **Systems** file is:

eagle Any ACU 300 957-1234 login--login nuucp ssword abcd123

The entry is for system "eagle" and will cause an 801 autodialer attached to a data set on a 300 baud line to dial 957−1234 and attempt to log in as "nuucp" with password "abcd123."

12.5.3 The Devices File

The **Devices** file is also contained in the **/usr/lib/uucp** directory. Its earlier name was **L-devices.** Each line specifies a hard wired line or autodialer/data set. The format of the line is

    line-name calling-unit-name speed

"Line" is the name of the special file for the line. "Calling-unit" is the name of the special file for the calling unit. "Speed" is the speed of the line in baud.

12.5.4 The Dialcodes File

The **Dialcodes** file is located in the **/usr/lib/uucp** directory. The former name for the file was **L-dialcodes.** The format of each line is:

    mnemonic dial-sequence

"Mnemonic" is a mnemonic abbreviation for a location. "Dial-sequence" is a phone number. Thus, the line

    nj 201

in the **Dialcodes** file causes the string

    nj 334-9999

in the **Systems** file to be translated to

201 334-9999

The translation takes place when *uucico* attempts to generate the phone number for a remote system in preparation for calling that system.

12.6 Setting Up *Uucp*

In this section, a general overview of setting up *uucp* will be presented. Each major specific action required to set up *uucp* will be discussed.

12.6.1 How to Create Password File Entries

Two logins are needed to implement *uucp*, traditionally called "nuucp" and "uucp." The "nuucp" login with login directory **/usr/spool/uucppublic** and */usr/lib/uucp/uucico* in the shell field is needed to enable remote systems to log into the local system.

A "uucp" login with login directory **/usr/lib/uucp** and a normal shell should be set up to take ownership of the *uucp* files and directories. The "uucp" files, directories, and programs should be owned by login "uucp" rather than "nuucp" in order to preserve local control and maintain a secure system.

12.6.2 How to Create Special Files

Recalling our assumption that we have an AT&T 801 autodialer and 212 data set installed, we might issue the following commands to set up the special files we need. We assume that the autodialer has major device number 1 and minor device number 0 and that the data set has major device number 7 and minor device number 0. These numbers are highly hardware and system dependent and are for illustrative purposes only. Consult your local site guide or customer engineer for specifics on your system.

```
mknod  /dev/cul0  c  1  0

chown  uucp  /dev/cul0

chmod  644  /dev/cul0



mknod  /dev/cua0  c  7  0

chown  uucp  /dev/cua0

chmod  644  /dev/cua0
```

12.6.3 How to Set Up /etc/inittab Entries for ACU Lines

Incoming *uucp* calls arrive on normal ports. Outgoing calls are placed only on ports associated with ACUs. Thus, the /etc/inittab action field entry for each of these ports must have the getty turned off.

12.6.4 How to Install *uucp* Software

Uucp is installed as part of the normal installation sequence. Parameters are set to default values. You can change the default parameters by editing the file **parms.h** and reinstall with the following command:

```
make -f uucp.mk install
```

12.6.5 How to Set Up *uucp* Files

The **Devices** file entry corresponding to the 801 autodialer and the 212 data set might be:

```
ACU cul0 cua0 300 801
```

The **Systems** and **Dialcodes** files are set up in the previously specified formats, based on whatever sites from which you want to receive calls and whatever sites you want to call **and** which are willing to communicate with you.

12.7 Security Considerations

The **Permissions** file (formerly **USERFILE**) is the key to *uucp* security. Permissions are explicitly granted. Default is to grant no remote execution capability and limit file transfer access to **/usr/spool/uucppublic**.

Sites not under your direct control should keep the default security limitations. Consider granting liberal privileges only to tightly coupled systems in your computer center. Having loose *uucp* security is like giving strangers logins on your system.

12.8 Solving User Problems

Two problems that users might have are inability to transmit to one or more remote systems and inability to receive from remote systems.

12.8.1 Inability to Receive

If the file system containing **/usr/spool/uucppublic** runs out of space, you will be unable to receive *uucp* jobs. You can verify that there is sufficient space in the **/usr** file system using the *df* command.

You can also verify that the "nuucp" login is set up by examining the **/etc/passwd** file. Manually logging into your system as "nuucp" can verify the existence of the login, the correct password, and the operation of the supporting hardware.

12.8.2 Inability to Transmit to All Destinations

An inability to transmit to all destinations can be a sign of bad data sets or autodialers on the local system. Bad hardware can be readily identified by examination of the status files or by using *cu* to dial out through each autodialer.

12.8.3 Inability to Transmit to a Small Number of Systems

An inability to transmit to a small number of systems may indicate hardware or administrative problems at those specific remote systems. By using *cu* to manually attempt to log into the problem sites, the problem can be narrowed down and the responsible system administrator(s) notified with a voice phone call.

Detailed information on the design and administration of *uucp* may be found in *UNIX Programmer's Manual, Vol. 2*, Bell Laboratories (Holt, Rinehart and Winston, 1983). In particular, anyone who is charged with administering *uucp* should read "A Dial-Up Network of UNIX Systems," by D. A. Nowitz and M. E. Lesk, and *"Uucp* Implementation Description," by D. A. Nowitz in the above book.

12.9 Summary

Uucp provides file transfer and remote execution capability among UNIX systems. It provides a user interface and executes work requests in the background.

A site with a single phone line and data set can be a passive site on the *uucp* network. With the addition of an autodialer, the site can become an active site and initiate a connection.

The user interfaces for file transmission and remote execution are called *uucp* and *uux*, respectively. Other programs execute in the background, namely *uucico* to execute data transmission requests, *uuxqt* to execute remote execution requests, *uulog* to manage the system log file, and *uuclean* to clean up work files after completion of work.

The **Systems** file lists system names that can be called and dialing instructions. The **Devices** file lists the phone lines and automatic calling units that are available. The **Dialcodes** file matches location names with phone numbers.

12.10 Exercises

1. Name the major features of a computer network.
2. Name the *uucp* user interface commands and explain what they are used for.

NETWORK ADMINISTRATION

3. What hardware is needed at a passive *uucp* site?
4. What hardware is needed at an active *uucp* site?
5. Describe the programs that implement *uucp* networking capability.
6. Name the major files used to implement *uucp* networking capability.
7. List and describe the fields in a **Systems** file entry.
8. List and describe the fields in a **Devices** file entry.
9. List and describe the fields in a **Dialcodes** file entry.
10. Discuss the security aspects of *uucp*.
11. Where would you look for detailed instruction on installing and maintaining *uucp* on your system?

13. ADMINISTERING CHANGE

OBJECTIVES

After reading this chapter, you should be able to:

1. Be familiar with the issues involved in converting to a new UNIX release.
2. Effectively plan for a hardware upgrade.
3. Be familiar with the issues involved in bringing up a new system.
4. Be familiar with the issues involved in planning a computer move.

A UNIX system changes with time. System administrators manage change on a continuing basis. This chapter explains how to manage change in UNIX systems.

13.1 Converting to a New UNIX Release

You need to do some planning to convert to a new UNIX release, after which you must implement both software porting and system conversion.

13.1.1 Planning

Major releases of SYSTEM V have historically been spaced 12–18 months apart. They are preceded by a *UNIX System Release Description*, which is a key document in planning for the new release. The document contains a summary of the features of the new release, instructions on how to install the new release, and a detailed list of changes in the new release.

It is my personal preference to convert to a new release of UNIX from 3 to 6 months after the official release. When UNIX release N comes out, the period of time that UNIX release N-1 will continue to be supported has typically been about a year. Support means that you can report bugs or ask for enhancements and expect the UNIX vendor to fix the bugs and to implement some of the enhancements requested by a significant number of sites. When support of a release is dropped by the vendor, you become the supporting organization. So, typically you want to convert to a new release before support is dropped for an old release.

13.1.2 Software Porting

You and your users have source programs that you will want to recompile and test and shell programs that you will want to test. Sometimes the source code of a program may need to be modified slightly to get the program to work properly. Such activities are called "software porting."

Sizing the Porting Job

The changes noted in the *System Release Description* must be analyzed in order to project the ease or difficulty of the porting job. The nature and number of programs in use on a system will also affect the magnitude of the job. Generally, shell programs are highly portable; source code changes are rarely needed.

Highly portable 'C' programs have the following characteristics:

1. They have makefiles that automate their installation.

2. Where possible, they use system utility subprograms to get a job done and make few assumptions about the structure of UNIX elements.

3. They do not make assumptions about the byte order or word length of the host hardware.

4. They do not make assumptions about system bugs, which may be fixed in the next release.

Providing Porting Resources

A technique to facilitate software porting is the installation of the 'C' compiler and shell from the new release on systems running the old release. These would be installed in a nonstandard directory like **/usr/new/bin**.

If a computer center has surplus computing resources, it may be possible to convert one of the existing systems to the new release for use in porting. Ongoing work would be transferred to other systems before conversion.

If a computer center is growing, it may be possible to bring up a new system with the new release of UNIX. This would allow thorough testing and would not disrupt ongoing work on other systems.

13.1.3 Conversion Scheduling

Installing a new release takes time. Both the system administrators and the end users need a period of time to port their programs to the new UNIX release. Time must be allowed to convert the first system to the new release and also to convert any other systems to the new release.

A system administrator should budget at least a full week of work time to install the new version of UNIX on the first system to be converted and to test that system. At least one day should be allotted to convert each subsequent system.

A substantial number of months may elapse from the time investigation into the new release is begun until the time that all systems have been cut over to it.

Table 13.1 shows a hypothetical conversion schedule. Roughly 3.5 months are allowed from the time the description of the release arrives until the first system is converted to the new release. During this time, planning, porting, and testing should take place. Seven months are allotted from the time the first system is converted until the time the last system is converted. Some users may have poorly written, hard-to-port code, or may be lax in their planning.

13.2 Augmenting Host Hardware

At some point you may need to upgrade your hardware. For example, you might want to install a new type of disk drive with higher storage capacity. Hardware basics will be presented first. Then, planning, scheduling, installing, and troubleshooting hardware upgrades will be discussed.

Table 13.1 New Release Conversion Schedule

Event	Date
Release description received	1/15
Conversion plan published	2/15
New compiler put up	3/1
New release run in system test time	4/1
First system converted	5/1
Last system converted	12/1

13.2.1 Hardware Basics

Most computer hardware resides in a cabinet. A cabinet is a metal box that has a cross section approximated by a square with 2.5-foot sides. Cabinets range from 3 to 6 feet high.

The contents of the cabinet depend on the type of hardware involved. A disk drive cabinet has one or more disk drive units. A tape drive cabinet has a tape drive unit. All cabinets have a power supply and at least one board carrier. The printed circuit boards contained in the carrier depend on the purpose of the hardware.

A board carrier holds one or more printed circuit boards in a fixed position. The boards are supplied with power and logical connections through a back plane at the rear of the board carrier. The back plane connects to other parts of the computer system through a bus or cable, which is essentially a group of wires.

A printed circuit board is the basic building block of a computer. Many people are already familiar with printed circuit boards through experience with personal computers. A board contains logic chips, printed wire connections between chips, a back plane connection, and other assorted electrical components. Many different kinds of boards exist, for example, cpu boards, memory boards, multiplexer boards, autodialer boards, and disk controller boards.

13.2.2 Planning

Considerable analysis must be part of planning a hardware upgrade. You should consider adding only hardware that is supported by your UNIX software vendor. Check to be sure that UNIX software support is available for the hardware you want to add.

You need to make physical arrangements for the upgraded hardware. Are floor space and power available for a new piece of equipment that comes in its own cabinet? Is there a suitable carrier slot available for new equipment that comes as a board or a set of boards?

13.2.3 Scheduling

New equipment is usually installed during system test time. Minor upgrades can be done on a weekday night. Major changes should be done on a Friday night, so that the whole weekend is available to either debug the new equipment or back it out.

13.2.4 Installation

Usually hardware is installed by the hardware vendor's technician. The system administrator will probably need to remake UNIX to configure the new hardware into the system. The new UNIX can be made ahead of time, and the old UNIX used until the new hardware is installed.

13.2.5 Troubleshooting

If the upgraded hardware does not work properly, check to see that you have the new equipment configured properly in UNIX and ask the hardware vendor's technician to check out the hardware. If you can't find the problem and the new hardware is not essential (an additional autodialer for example), you could go back to your old version of UNIX and have the system ignore the new hardware. If you can't find the problem and the new hardware is essential (a faster cpu for example), either the problem must be escalated to a higher technical level or the new hardware must be backed out.

13.3 Bringing Up New Host Hardware

We will now examine the situation in which you want to bring up a new computer system. The new computer might be an additional system of a type that you already have, or it might be a make and model that has never been installed in your computer center. Planning, scheduling, installation, porting, and troubleshooting will be discussed.

13.3.1 Planning

Obtaining a new computer and in particular a new type of computer, is a major change for a computer center. Introducing the new hardware must be carefully planned. Usually, a thorough study is conducted, a draft plan circulated to affected personnel, and ultimately a final plan published on how the new hardware will be put into production.

When considering a new type of system, a key question to ask is whether a supported version of UNIX is available.

13.3.2 Scheduling

The new equipment must be installed and successfully tested before it is needed in production. It can typically take several months to define the need for a new computer and obtain management authorization, several months to obtain the hardware, and several months to install and test the hardware. If this type of system has never before been used in your computer center, a software porting effort will be involved. This work can all be done on prime shift. The final step of transferring users to the new system should be done in system test time.

13.3.3 Installation

Vendor technicians install the new computer. The computer center supplies space, suitable power, and other utilities. The system administrator makes a UNIX for the new system and tests the system.

13.3.4 Porting

User software must be ported whenever a new kind of computer is installed in a computer center for the first time. Shell programs will probably run on the new computer without change. Programs written in 'C' that do not make assumptions about the word size or byte order of the underlying hardware and that have makefiles should port easily. Otherwise, the porting effort could be substantial.

13.3.5 Troubleshooting

Troubleshooting new equipment can be a challenge. If you are lucky, you have good vendor support for the new hardware and software. Having contacts at a facility that already has a system of the same type running can be very helpful. Since a new computer is not yet in production, troubleshooting does not usually take on crisis proportions as frequently as does troubleshooting of production equipment.

13.4 Moving Computers

Sometimes a computer needs to be moved a few feet within a computer center to accommodate other equipment. Sometimes a computer needs to be moved to a new computer center. Both situations require careful planning and implementation.

Moving a computer involves planning, scheduling, premove preparation, moving, and postmove troubleshooting.

13.4.1 Planning

A minor move within a computer center may be planned informally. A major move involving relocation to a new building should have a written plan, with affected parties given the opportunity to comment while the plan is in draft form. Areas that should be dealt with in the plan are space, power, environmental requirements, move-related downtime, scheduling the move, and arrangements for the move.

13.4.2 Scheduling

A major move should be scheduled at a time that minimizes adverse impact on users. Generally, you should move immediately before a weekend so that most of the downtime for moving and reinstallation of equipment takes place during off prime shift. Experienced hardware technicians can break down and reinstall a minicomputer in two days and a moderate-sized mainframe in four days, provided the site has been properly prepared in the destination computer center.

13.4.3 Preparation

Space in the destination computer center must be available for the equipment being moved. Power, appropriate climate control, and data communications resources should all be available and tested in the destination computer center before the move is begun.

If the move is a multi-computer move that is to take place over several weekends, the user organization of each computer and the actual users of each computer must be identified and provision made for either moving a computer and its user community together or at least providing telecommunications access for the user community. Load balancing may be required to get users on their organization's computer.

13.4.4 Moving

Hardware vendor technicians must be brought in to break down the computer hardware at the source computer center. Computer movers implement the move. The hardware vendors reinstall the computers in the destination computer center, and finally the system administrator boots the system and checks it out. The system administrator should be present during the breakdown and reinstallation of the system to handle unexpected problems.

13.4.5 Troubleshooting

Change always involves risk. System administration personnel must be ready to handle problems that arise immediately after a move. It is impossible to predict all the problems that may arise during a move, but some typical problems are poor data communications lines, and *uucp* not being able to dial out in the new data communications environment.

13.5 Summary

A system administrator must learn to manage change. UNIX software and the underlying hardware is subject to change. Further, from time to time it may be necessary to relocate the hardware.

Approximately every year and a half you will need to install a new UNIX release. The release will be preceded by a *UNIX System Release Description,* which documents the changes introduced in the release and the installation procedure for the release. In a computer center with reserve computing capacity or in a growing computer center, an unloaded system can be brought up on the new UNIX release and used for software porting. Otherwise, the compilers and shell from the new UNIX release could be put up on a system running the old release and porting done there.

From time to time you may want to install additional hardware. Some analysis needs to be done to be sure UNIX and your existing hardware can support the new hardware.

With the rapid pace of technology change, you may need to replace existing hardware with more powerful hardware. For example, you may want to replace a 16 bit word size PDP11 with a 32 bit word size 3B20. You must bring a prototype new system up well before users are cut over to it and provide them with an adequate opportunity to port their software to the new system.

If your organization moves, you will have to move your hardware. A computer move must be studied and a written plan published that documents the various aspects of the move. The move should be implemented immediately before a weekend to allow adequate time to get the hardware working in the new location before it is needed by users.

13.6 Exercises

1. Discuss the pros and cons of converting immediately to a new UNIX release.
2. Where do you find out about a new UNIX release?
3. Describe a potential scenario for installing a new release of UNIX in a computer center with several systems.
4. Describe a potential scenario for installing a new release of UNIX in a computer center with one system.
5. What is meant by software porting?
6. What kind of programs port most easily? What kind of programs port less easily?
7. Should you make assumptions about the word size and byte order of a computer when you are writing programs? Why or why not?
8. What is a cabinet, a carrier, and a board?
9. What analysis should you do before you order a new piece of hardware?

ADMINISTERING CHANGE 167

10. Name some important aspects of a computer move that require planning. When during the week is the best time to implement a computer move?

11. What are the responsibilities of the hardware vendor, the mover, and the system administrator in a computer move?

APPENDIX A: REFERENCES

1. **C LANGUAGE**

    A. *The C Programming Language*, B. Kernighan and D. Ritchie, Prentice-Hall, 1978.

    B. *UNIX SYSTEM V Programmer Reference Manual*, AT&T Bell Laboratories, 1983.

2. **DATA COMMUNICATIONS**

    A. *Technical Aspects of Data Communications, 2nd ed.*, J. McNamara, Digital Press, 1982.

3. **SHELL**

    A. *The UNIX Programming Environment*, B. Kernighan and R. Pike, Prentice-Hall, 1984.

    B. *UNIX SYSTEM V Release 2 User Reference Manual*, AT&T Bell Laboratories, December 1983.

4. **SYSTEM ADMINISTRATION OF MINICOMPUTERS**

    A. *UNIX SYSTEM V Administrator Reference Manual*, AT&T Bell Laboratories, December 1983.

    B. *UNIX SYSTEM V Release 2 Administrator Guide for 3B20 Computers*, Western Electric Co., 1983.

    C. *UNIX SYSTEM V Release 2 System Release Description for 3B20S Computers*, Western Electric Co., 1983.

5. **SYSTEM ADMINISTRATION OF PERSONAL COMPUTERS**

    A. *AT&T UNIX PC Model 7300 Getting Started Guide*, AT&T, 1985.

B. *AT&T UNIX PC Model 7300 Owner's Manual,* AT&T, 1985.

C. *Quick Reference Guide - Managing the UNIX PC,* AT&T, 1985.

D. *Quick Reference Guide - Owner's Manual (for the UNIX PC),* AT&T, 1985.

APPENDIX B: MANUAL PAGES REFERENCED

1. Manual pages referenced in the *UNIX SYSTEM V USER REFERENCE MANUAL*
   - A. *cpio*
   - B. *crypt*
   - C. *dd*
   - D. *du*
   - E. *echo*
   - F. *find*
   - G. *kill*
   - H. *ls*
   - I. *mail*
   - J. *make*
   - K. *newgrp*
   - L. *passwd*
   - M. *ps*
   - N. *rm*
   - O. *sar*
   - P. *sh*
   - Q. *sync*
   - R. *uucp*
   - S. *who*

2. Manual pages referenced in the *UNIX SYSTEM V Programmer Reference Manual*

   A. **gettydefs**
   B. **inittab**
   C. **system**

3. Manual pages referenced in the *UNIX SYSTEM V Administrator Reference Manual*
   A. *config*
   B. *cron*
   C. *dcopy*
   D. *df*
   E. *fsck*
   F. *getty*
   G. *init*
   H. *labelit*
   I. *login*
   J. *mkfs*
   K. *mount (umount)*
   L. *setmnt*
   M. *volcopy*

INDEX

.profile file 28
/etc/checklist file 81
/etc/gettydefs file 43
/etc/group file format 92
/etc/inittab file 42
/etc/profile file 91
/etc/rc command 82
/etc/shutdown command 82
3B20S computer, configuration 132
3B20S computer, function keys 134
3B20S computer, interface 133
3B20S computer, overview 132
3B20S computer, screen areas 134
ASCII code 48
RS232C interface 40
UMASK 91
UNIX, booting 136
UNIX, distribution tapes 135
UNIX, initial loading of 135
UNIX, making 142
UNIX, release conversion 158
UNIX, release planning 158
acctcms command 108
asynchronous communication 36
autodialer 151
back plane 161
backup methodology choice 83
baud 42
bid procedures 127
bid specification 124
block 51
block size 105
break out boxes 41
broadcast message 12
byte 48
cabinet 161
central processing unit 118
checklist file 59
clear to send pin on RS232C interface 41

computer center, private 7
computer center, public 7
computer room security 99
computer system selection 22
configuration specification 125
contract procedures 127
conventions, syntax 4
conversion scheduling 160
cpu, activity monitoring 113
cpu, cycle shortage 115
cpu, usage monitoring 106
crash 85
cron command 84
crypt command 95
data communications, equipment 40
data communications, overview 36
data communications, problems 44
data set ready pin on RS232C interface 41
data sets 40
data terminal equipment 40
date command 81
dcopy command 62
device numbers 139
df command 105
directory 49
directory, modes 91
disaster 85
disk drive, activity monitoring 113
disk drive, overview 119
disk, block size 105
disk, free space monitoring 105
disk, space shortage 114
du command 105
electronic mail, packages 10
electronic mail, sending 11
emergencies 85
file, backup 78, 83
file, encryption 95
file, implementation 51

INDEX

file, modes 91
file, regular 48
file, restoral 61, 84
file, special 50
file system, backup 59
file system, creation 55
file system, device format 54
file system, disk drive mapping 55
file system, fragmented 62
file system, full 61
file system, full volume copy 60
file system, hierarchical 49
file system, incremental copy 60
file system, initial set up 55
file system, mount point 57
file system, mounting 57
file system, overview 51
file system, quiescing 83
file system, sanity checking 58
file system, selection 22
file system, unmounting 57
free list 52
free space monitoring 105
fsck command 59
full duplex communication 36
getty process 37
group ID 25
groups 92
hard shutdown 83
hardware, augmentation 160
hardware, bringing up new 162
hardware, configuration 117
hardware, upgrade 79
init command 82
init process 37
initial load, /usr file system 137
initial load, selectable items 137
inode 52
inumber 49
kill command 73
labelit command 56
local area network 121
login directory, creation 28
login directory, overview 26
login management 97
login name 24
login shell 26
login, authorization 20
login, deletion shell 32
login, handling problems 32
login, in multi-computer center 29
login, in single computer center 29
login, removal automation 32
login, removing 31

login, request form 20
login, setup 19
login, setup shell 29
mail command 11
mailx command 12
major device number 50
memory, overview 118
memory, shortage 115
message of the day 8
minor device number 50
mnttab file 57
mount point 57
mount command 58
moving computers, overview 164
moving computers, physical move 165
moving computers, planning 164
moving computers, scheduling 164
moving computers, site preparation 164
moving computers, troubleshooting 165
multi-user mode transition 81
multiplexer, overview 120
multiplexer, ports 39
networking hardware 120
newgrp command 93
news -a command 10
news -n command 9
news command 8
newsletter 15
null modems 42
off prime shift 78
operational schedule, design 77
operational schedule, example 80
operations room 16
operator, duties of 1
operator, education 86
operator, skills 86
operator, training 86
password aging 97
password file entry, creation 23
password file, structure 23
password security 97
password, expiration 25
password, field 24
port, monitoring 109
port, plan 109
port, shortage 114
port, usage monitoring 111
portable source code 159
preventive maintenance 79
prime shift 78
printed circuit board 161

INDEX

printers 121
process accounting, data gathering 106
process accounting, record format 107
process, creation 67
process, monitoring 69
process, overview 66
process, response to a signal 68
ps -a command 73
ps -e command 73
ps -p command 73
ps -u command 73
ps command 69
received data pin on RS232C interface 40
received line signal detect pin on RS232C 41
request to send pin on RS232C interface 40
resource administration 104
sar command 112
security automation 95
shell process 37
signal ground pin on RS232C interface 40
signals 68
single-user mode 80
site preparation 127
software drivers 141
software porting, overview 159
software porting, resources for 159
software porting, sizing 159
software, upgrade 79
special files, description 138
special files, examining 140
special files, making 140
special files, types of 138
subdirectories 29
superblock 53
superuser control 96
system administrator, duties of 1
system administrator, prerequisites 3
system description file 141
system generation, documentation 132
system generation, hardware dependence 131
system generation, prerequisites 133
system generation, procedures 131
system parameters 141
system programmer, duties of 2

tape drive, activity monitoring 113
tape drive, overview 119
tape production control 99
telecommunications control 98
transmission medium 40
transmission method, choice of 13
transmitted data pin on RS232C interface 40
user ID 25
user orientation 29
users, counseling 15
users, education 16
users, training 16
uucico program 149
uuclean program 150
uucp command 146
uucp command overview 145
uucp **Devices** file 152
uucp **Dialcodes** file 152
uucp **Systems** file 150
uucp hardware overview 148
uucp problem solving 155
uucp security considerations 155
uucp set up 153
uucp software installation 154
uucp spooling directory 150
uulog command 148
uuname command 147
uustat command 147
uux command 146
uuxqt program 150
vendor evaluation 127
volcopy command 60
wall command 12
wide area network 120